Michelle Bachelet

MODERN WORLD LEADERS

Michelle Bachelet

Tony Blair

George W. Bush

Hugo Chávez

Jacques Chirac

Hu Jintao

Hamid Karzai

Ali Khamenei

Thabo Mbeki

Angela Merkel

Hosni Mubarak

Pervez Musharraf

Pope Benedict XVI

Pope John Paul II

Vladimir Putin

The Saudi Royal Family

Ariel Sharon

Viktor Yushchenko

MODERN WORLD LEADERS

Michelle Bachelet

Richard Worth

Michelle Bachelet

Chelsea House
An imprint of Infobase Publishing
132 West 31st Street
New York, NY 10001

Library of Congress Cataloging-in-Publication Data

Worth, Richard.
  Michelle Bachelet / Richard Worth.
     p. cm. — (Modern world leaders)
  Includes bibliographical references and index.
  ISBN-13: 978-0-7910-9500-3 (hardcover)
  ISBN-10: 0-7910-9500-2 (hardcover)
  1. Bachelet, Michelle, 1951- 2. Chile—Politics and government—20th century. 3. Women presidents—Chile. I. Title. II. Series.
  F3101.4.B33W67 2007
  983.06'4092—dc22
  [B]   2007000897

Chelsea House books are available at special discounts when purchased in bulk quantities for businesses, associations, institutions, or sales promotions. Please call our Special Sales Department in New York at (212) 967-8800 or (800) 322-8755.

You can find Chelsea House on the World Wide Web at http://www.chelseahouse.com

Text design by Erik Lindstrom
Cover design by Takeshi Takahashi

Printed in the United States of America

Bang FOF 10 9 8 7 6 5 4 3 2 1

This book is printed on acid-free paper.

All links and Web addresses were checked and verified to be correct at the time of publication. Because of the dynamic nature of the Web, some addresses and links may have changed since publication and may no longer be valid.

TABLE OF CONTENTS

On Leadership

Leadership, it may be said, is really what makes the world go round. Love no doubt smoothes the passage; but love is a private transaction between consenting adults. Leadership is a public transaction with history. The idea of leadership affirms the capacity of individuals to move, inspire, and mobilize masses of people so that they act together in pursuit of an end. Sometimes leadership serves good purposes, sometimes bad; but whether the end is benign or evil, great leaders are those men and women who leave their personal stamp on history.

Now, the very concept of leadership implies the proposition that individuals can make a difference. This proposition has never been universally accepted. From classical times to the present day, eminent thinkers have regarded individuals as no more than the agents and pawns of larger forces, whether the gods and goddesses of the ancient world or, in the modern era, race, class, nation, the dialectic, the will of the people, the spirit of the times, history itself. Against such forces, the individual dwindles into insignificance.

So contends the thesis of historical determinism. Tolstoy's great novel *War and Peace* offers a famous statement of the case. Why, Tolstoy asked, did millions of men in the Napoleonic Wars, denying their human feelings and their common sense, move back and forth across Europe slaughtering their fellows? "The war," Tolstoy answered, "was bound to happen simply because it was bound to happen." All prior history determined it. As for leaders, they, Tolstoy said, "are but the labels that serve to give a name to an end and, like labels, they have the least possible connection with the event." The greater the leader, "the more conspicuous the inevitability and the predestination of every act he commits." The leader, said Tolstoy, is "the slave of history."

Determinism takes many forms. Marxism is the determinism of class. Nazism the determinism of race. But the idea of men and women as the slaves of history runs athwart the deepest human instincts. Rigid determinism abolishes the idea of human freedom—the assumption of free choice that underlies every move we make, every word we speak, every thought we think. It abolishes the idea of human responsibility, since it is manifestly unfair to reward or punish people for actions that are by definition beyond their control. No one can live consistently by any deterministic creed. The Marxist states prove this themselves by their extreme susceptibility to the cult of leadership.

More than that, history refutes the idea that individuals make no difference. In December 1931, a British politician crossing Fifth Avenue in New York City between 76th and 77th streets around 10:30 P.M. looked in the wrong direction and was knocked down by an automobile—a moment, he later recalled, of a man aghast, a world aglare: "I do not understand why I was not broken like an eggshell or squashed like a gooseberry." Fourteen months later an American politician, sitting in an open car in Miami, Florida, was fired on by an assassin; the man beside him was hit. Those who believe that individuals make no difference to history might well ponder whether the next two decades would have been the same had Mario Constasino's car killed Winston Churchill in 1931 and Giuseppe Zangara's bullet killed Franklin Roosevelt in 1933. Suppose, in addition, that Lenin had died of typhus in Siberia in 1895 and that Hitler had been killed on the western front in 1916. What would the twentieth century have looked like now?

For better or for worse, individuals do make a difference. "The notion that a people can run itself and its affairs anonymously," wrote the philosopher William James, "is now well known to be the silliest of absurdities. Mankind does nothing save through initiatives on the part of inventors, great or small, and imitation by the rest of us—these are the sole factors in human progress. Individuals of genius show the way, and set the patterns, which common people then adopt and follow."

Leadership, James suggests, means leadership in thought as well as in action. In the long run, leaders in thought may well make the greater difference to the world. "The ideas of economists and political philosophers, both when they are right and when they are wrong," wrote John Maynard Keynes, "are more powerful than is commonly understood. Indeed the world is ruled by little else. Practical men, who believe themselves to be quite exempt from any intellectual influences, are usually the slaves of some defunct economist. . . . The power of vested interests is vastly exaggerated compared with the gradual encroachment of ideas."

But, as Woodrow Wilson once said, "Those only are leaders of men, in the general eye, who lead in action. . . . It is at their hands that new thought gets its translation into the crude language of deeds." Leaders in thought often invent in solitude and obscurity, leaving to later generations the tasks of imitation. Leaders in action—the leaders portrayed in this series—have to be effective in their own time.

And they cannot be effective by themselves. They must act in response to the rhythms of their age. Their genius must be adapted, in a phrase from William James, "to the receptivities of the moment." Leaders are useless without followers. "There goes the mob," said the French politician, hearing a clamor in the streets. "I am their leader. I must follow them." Great leaders turn the inchoate emotions of the mob to purposes of their own. They seize on the opportunities of their time, the hopes, fears, frustrations, crises, potentialities. They succeed when events have prepared the way for them, when the community is awaiting to be aroused, when they can provide the clarifying and organizing ideas. Leadership completes the circuit between the individual and the mass and thereby alters history.

It may alter history for better or for worse. Leaders have been responsible for the most extravagant follies and most monstrous crimes that have beset suffering humanity. They have also been vital in such gains as humanity has made in individual freedom, religious and racial tolerance, social justice, and respect for human rights.

There is no sure way to tell in advance who is going to lead for good and who for evil. But a glance at the gallery of men and women in MODERN WORLD LEADERS suggests some useful tests.

One test is this: Do leaders lead by force or by persuasion? By command or by consent? Through most of history leadership was exercised by the divine right of authority. The duty of followers was to defer and to obey. "Theirs not to reason why/Theirs but to do and die." On occasion, as with the so-called enlightened despots of the eighteenth century in Europe, absolutist leadership was animated by humane purposes. More often, absolutism nourished the passion for domination, land, gold, and conquest and resulted in tyranny.

The great revolution of modern times has been the revolution of equality. "Perhaps no form of government," wrote the British historian James Bryce in his study of the United States, *The American Commonwealth*, "needs great leaders so much as democracy." The idea that all people should be equal in their legal condition has undermined the old structure of authority, hierarchy, and deference. The revolution of equality has had two contrary effects on the nature of leadership. For equality, as Alexis de Tocqueville pointed out in his great study *Democracy in America*, might mean equality in servitude as well as equality in freedom.

"I know of only two methods of establishing equality in the political world," Tocqueville wrote. "Rights must be given to every citizen, or none at all to anyone . . . save one, who is the master of all." There was no middle ground "between the sovereignty of all and the absolute power of one man." In his astonishing prediction of twentieth-century totalitarian dictatorship, Tocqueville explained how the revolution of equality could lead to the *Führerprinzip* and more terrible absolutism than the world had ever known.

But when rights are given to every citizen and the sovereignty of all is established, the problem of leadership takes a new form, becomes more exacting than ever before. It is easy to issue commands and enforce them by the rope and the stake, the concentration camp and the *gulag*. It is much harder to use argument and achievement to overcome opposition and win consent. The Founding Fathers of the United States understood the difficulty. They believed that history had given them the opportunity to decide, as Alexander Hamilton wrote in the first Federalist Paper, whether men are indeed capable of basing government on "reflection and choice, or whether they are forever destined to depend . . . on accident and force."

Government by reflection and choice called for a new style of leadership and a new quality of followership. It required leaders to be responsive to popular concerns, and it required followers to be active and informed participants in the process. Democracy does not eliminate emotion from politics; sometimes it fosters demagoguery; but it is confident that, as the greatest of democratic leaders put it, you cannot fool all of the people all of the time. It measures leadership by results and retires those who overreach or falter or fail.

It is true that in the long run despots are measured by results too. But they can postpone the day of judgment, sometimes indefinitely, and in the meantime they can do infinite harm. It is also true that democracy is no guarantee of virtue and intelligence in government, for the voice of the people is not necessarily the voice of God. But democracy, by assuring the right of opposition, offers built-in resistance to the evils inherent in absolutism. As the theologian Reinhold Niebuhr summed it up, "Man's capacity for justice makes democracy possible, but man's inclination to justice makes democracy necessary."

A second test for leadership is the end for which power is sought. When leaders have as their goal the supremacy of a master race or the promotion of totalitarian revolution or the acquisition and exploitation of colonies or the protection of greed and privilege or the preservation of personal power, it is likely that their leadership will do little to advance the cause of humanity. When their goal is the abolition of slavery, the liberation of women, the enlargement of opportunity for the poor and powerless, the extension of equal rights to racial minorities, the defense of the freedoms of expression and opposition, it is likely that their leadership will increase the sum of human liberty and welfare.

Leaders have done great harm to the world. They have also conferred great benefits. You will find both sorts in this series. Even "good" leaders must be regarded with a certain wariness. Leaders are not demigods; they put on their trousers one leg after another just like ordinary mortals. No leader is infallible, and every leader needs to be reminded of this at regular intervals. Irreverence irritates leaders but is their salvation. Unquestioning submission corrupts leaders and demeans followers. Making a cult of a leader is always a mistake. Fortunately hero worship generates its own antidote. "Every hero," said Emerson, "becomes a bore at last."

The single benefit the great leaders confer is to embolden the rest of us to live according to our own best selves, to be active, insistent, and resolute in affirming our own sense of things. For great leaders attest to the reality of human freedom against the supposed inevitabilities of history. And they attest to the wisdom and power that may lie within the most unlikely of us, which is why Abraham Lincoln remains the supreme example of great leadership. A great leader, said Emerson, exhibits new possibilities to all humanity. "We feed on genius. . . . Great men exist that there may be greater men."

Great leaders, in short, justify themselves by emancipating and empowering their followers. So humanity struggles to master its destiny, remembering with Alexis de Tocqueville: "It is true that around every man a fatal circle is traced beyond which he cannot pass; but within the wide verge of that circle he is powerful and free; as it is with man, so with communities." ●

1

President of Chile

"I THINK I CAN DO POLITICS DIFFERENTLY BECAUSE I AM A WOMAN," THE candidate told a large crowd of voters, according to a March 2006 article in *Progressive* by Alfonso Daniels. "People expect women to be more ethical and caring than men." Dr. Michelle Bachelet, 53 years old and Chile's former defense minister, was running for president of her country. If she won, Bachelet would become the first woman to be elected to the presidency in Chile. Indeed, she would become one of the few women in the world to hold the prestigious position of running a nation.

Chile is in South America. It is a long, narrow country that runs along the Pacific coast, from Peru in the north to the southern tip of the South American continent. The capital, Santiago, is centrally located in the country and is one of the biggest cities in South America. Chile has a long history of democracy, stretching back into the nineteenth century. In

When she was elected president of Chile in 2006, Michelle Bachelet became the first woman to ever hold that position, as well as becoming one of few female leaders in the world. In the photograph above, Michelle Bachelet greets an indigenous Chilean woman during her presidential campaign in 2005.

1973, however, the democratically elected president was overthrown by the Chilean army.

For almost 20 years, Chileans lived under a brutal dictatorship. Bachelet's father died in prison; she and her mother were tortured during the dictatorship and fled to Eastern Europe. "I'm not an angel," she was quoted as saying in a January 4, 2003, story in *The New York Times*, at a time when she was the country's defense minister. "I haven't forgotten. It left pain. But I have tried to channel the pain into a constructive realm. I insist on the idea that what happened here in Chile was so painful, so terrible, that I wouldn't wish for anyone to live through our situation again."

After returning to Chile, Bachelet, a pediatrician, joined the struggle to remove that dictatorship. After democracy was restored in the 1990s, she worked in the public health field—winning an outstanding reputation for her efforts to help reduce disease among the poor. She became an expert in defense policies, especially the relationship between the army and the civilian government. Meanwhile, she also committed herself to preventing the Chilean military from ever again overthrowing her country's democracy. "One day," she recalled in Daniels's 2006 article in *Progressive*, "I was walking with my mother and we bumped into [one of her torturers]. We identified ourselves, and what we saw next was a human being who was crying and lacked the courage to look in our eyes. A completely diminished character carrying a bag filled with guilt."

A new president, Ricardo Lagos, was elected in 1999, and he appointed Bachelet as his administration's minister of health. Widely popular among the Chilean people, Bachelet was transferred in 2002 to an even more important position—minister of defense. Bachelet was the first woman to become a defense minister in South America.

As Lagos's term neared expiration, his party began looking for potential candidates. With a broad appeal and a wide range of experience, Bachelet was on one hand an attractive choice. As Daniels wrote, "since she was a popular figure in the cabinet of Ricardo Lagos . . . a group of senators invited her to a secret meeting in a Santiago apartment to see if she was interested in the party nomination." They knew that Bachelet was also an unusual candidate. In addition to being a woman, which would make her a rarity in Chilean politics, Bachelet was also a divorced, single mother with three children. Chile is a conservative country, where women have traditionally put home and family ahead of careers. Nevertheless, as Bachelet was quick to point out in an April 2, 2005, article in the *Economist*, "I am an ordinary person. . . . I have a different sort of family, but one that is similar to a third of Chilean families."

Like other single mothers, she did the shopping, carried out household chores, and supported her family while taking her children to school every morning before beginning work. "People see me," she told interviewer Jonathan Franklin for a November 20, 2005, article in *Women's eNews*. "I am a mother, head of household," like many other women. "Today in Chile, one third of households are run by women. We wake up, get the children ready and go to work. To them, I am hope."

PREPARING TO RUN

Bachelet held focus groups with Chilean voters to make sure she understood what most concerned them. The nation has one of the largest gaps between rich and poor of any country in the world. The poor have a life span that is 15 to 20 years shorter than well-to-do Chileans. In addition, as noted in a March 2006 article in *Contemporary Review*, most children attend public schools, where spending is only 20 percent as much as it is in private schools for the children of the wealthy.

Expanding on her long commitment to public health, Bachelet decided to concentrate her campaign on redressing the imbalances in Chilean society. "We need to balance political stability, economic growth, and successful social policies," she announced during her campaign, according to Daniels's March 2006 article in *Progressive*. "This also implies reducing inequality in our education, providing greater government assistance, and encouraging entrepreneurship."

When she hit the campaign trail in early 2005, Bachelet met wide support among Chilean voters. Her own life experience helped people who had been left out of the booming economy feel that they might become part of Chile's future. "Michelle makes you feel like we did it together," a woman who worked with Bachelet when she was health minister told Franklin for his *Women's eNews* article. "The other day I went to a birthday party with 15 women and 10 men. They were all talking about Michelle Bachelet and her magic. She is awakening the idea that we need a new style of politics. . . . She generates confidence."

Among her major campaign themes was changing the Chilean pension system. Under that system, most retirees received less than $140 per month to live. Bachelet promised to improve the system if she were elected. She also committed to making improvements in the public education and health care systems. "We should continue to grow economically, that is very important," Bachelet said in a January 2006 article in *Maclean's*, "but we have to make sure that everybody in this country will have the benefits of growth."

THE ELECTION CAMPAIGN

Early in the 2005 presidential campaign, Bachelet held a wide lead in public opinion polls. As the candidate of the ruling party, the center-left Coalition of Parties for Democracy, she had the support of more than 48 percent of voters—far more than her three opponents in the race. Among them was Joaquín Lavín, the candidate of the Independent Democratic Union (UDI), a right-wing party. He had run for president in 1999, narrowly losing to Lagos. A second candidate was billionaire industrialist Sebastián Piñera. He was nominated by the National Renewal party (RN), a center-right political group. Piñera owned a major television station in Chile as well as a large part of the Chilean national airline. The third candidate was Tomas Hirsch, an engineer, representing several leftist parties. Hirsch had also run in the 1999 presidential campaign.

During her presidential campaign, Bachelet focused on issues such as improving public education and health care services. Above, Bachelet participates in a 2005 televised presidential debate with candidate Sebastian Piñera. During the presidential debates, Bachelet was criticized for her shaky and nervous performance.

As the campaign heated up, the candidates held a series of debates. As the *Economist* magazine reported December 10, 2005, Bachelet "performed nervously in all three television debates. She has yet to master the crisp soundbite. That halting performance may have caused some voters to have second thoughts about having a woman as president." In addition, Piñera was spending vast amounts of his own money for media coverage that helped him gain wider support.

As election time neared in December 2005, Bachelet had dropped in the polls, which were predicting that she might carry 41 percent of the vote. Nevertheless, she was still outdistancing Piñera and Lavín. The best they could hope to do was to prevent her from winning 50 percent of the vote, the amount necessary to be elected president. This would necessitate a runoff election in January 2006.

In early December, with the election nearing, Bachelet reminded voters that she was different than the other candidates. "I'm With You" was her slogan. She was one of the people. Marta Lagos, a Chilean pollster, was quoted in a December 10, 2005, article by the Washington Post Foreign Service as saying, "She's already doing things in a different way, and people have criticized her harshly for it. She has a daughter, and in September they took a few days off and went to the beach in the middle of the campaign. It's unthinkable for any politician to say, 'I'm with my family, and this is my time—no one else's.' But that's what she said."

At a campaign rally just before the election, Bachelet strummed a guitar, an instrument she had learned to play as a youth. She acknowledged that she was not the typical candidate. In a nation that is heavily Catholic, Bachelet is an agnostic—someone who believes that God cannot be known and who has no traditional religious beliefs. "I'm agnostic. . . . I believe in the state. I believe the state has an important role in guaranteeing the diversity of men and women in Chile—their different spiritualities, philosophies and ways of life," she said in the Washington Post Foreign Service article.

THE ELECTION RESULTS

On December 11, 2005, Chile's voters went to the polls. Michelle Bachelet finished first with 46 percent of the vote, while Piñera finished a distant second. Under Chilean law, Bachelet and Piñera moved on to the second round of voting in January 2006. To ensure that she received a majority of votes in that round, the leaders of Coalition of Parties for Democracy "threw themselves into the campaign in defense

Michelle Bachelet greets her supporters after she was sworn in as president of Chile on March 11, 2006. In the December 11 elections, Bachelet won 46 percent of the vote with Piñera finishing a distant second. In Chile, in order to win the presidency a candidate must receive absolute majority of the vote, and so Bachelet and Piñera entered a runoff election in January 2006. Bachelet won 53.5 percent of the vote and became Chile's new president.

of their candidate," according to reporter Carlos Malamud in a March 7, 2006, article on NuevaMayoria.com. "This unbroken support . . . was massively joined by President Lagos and the entire government." Lagos was a popular president with a high approval rating, and he carried enormous influence with voters. Piñera had the support of Lavín and the UDI. With the combined support, he hoped to defeat Bachelet.

During the campaign, Bachelet vowed to continue Lagos's successful economic policies and to reduce the unemployment rate in Chile, which stood at nine percent. She reaffirmed her commitment to improving the lives of Chile's poor. On January 15, 2006, Chile's voters cast their ballots in the runoff. As the returns poured in, Bachelet supporters realized that their candidate had been elected president. She won more than 53 percent of the vote.

On the night of her triumph, Bachelet appeared before cheering supporters in Santiago. She was the first woman to become president of a Latin-American nation whose husband had not been president or prominent in politics. As one of her supporters, Karina Melendez, told Inter Press Service News Agency for an article on January 16, 2006, "I never would have dreamed that this could happen." And Bachelet echoed these words in her address to about 200,000 supporters after her victory.

"Who would have thought 20, 10, or even five years ago that Chile would elect a woman as president? It seemed highly unlikely, but it was possible. It is possible, because the citizens of the country wanted it. Because democracy allowed it," she said in the Inter Press Service report.

In her victory speech, as reported on January 25, 2006, on Online News Hour, she struck a theme that had carried her through the campaign. "Because I was the victim of hate, I've consecrated my life to turning hate into understanding, tolerance, and why not say it—love." As president, Michelle Bachelet hoped to begin a new chapter in Chile's history.

CHAPTER

2

Legacy from the Past

THE LONG, NARROW COUNTRY OF CHILE STRETCHES FOR 2,600 MILES ALONG the western coast of South America. It lies between the Pacific Ocean and the high Andes mountains to the east. This range contains Aconcagua and Nevado Ojos del Salado, the highest mountains in the Western Hemisphere. In the northern part of Chile is the barren Atacama Desert, along the border with Peru. Atacama is about 100 miles wide and considered the driest desert on the globe. Very little rain reaches the Atacama Desert because the winds that bring moist air from the east coast rise up over the Andes and drop their moisture before reaching the desert. Central Chile is a lush valley with several rivers and dense forests, while the south is a much colder region that includes Cape Horn—part of Chile—on the tip of South America. In the Pacific Ocean are several islands that form part of Chile. Among them is Easter Island, with its more than 800 large stone sculptures. Chile is located in area where one of the

The above illustration depicts the indigenous Araucanian Indians who inhabited Chile during the end of the fifteenth century. The Araucanians were farmers and hunters, as well as skilled warriors. They inhabited Chile prior to the arrival of the Incas and the Spaniards.

large plates that form part of the Earth's crust is moving under another plate. As a result, earthquakes are common—28 large quakes occurred in Chile during the twentieth century.

INDIANS OF CHILE

By the last part of the fifteenth century, Chile was home to approximately one million Araucanian Indians. They included three different tribal people—the Picunche who lived in the northern areas, the Choapa, who inhabited the central valley, and the Mapuche, who lived in central Chile and in the far south. The Araucanians were farmers who grew a variety of crops, including *maize* (corn), beans, and potatoes. They wore clothing woven from the wool of llamas. These large animals, which look something like camels, were also used by the Indians to transport baggage weighing as much as 100 pounds.

During the late fifteenth century, the Picunche in the north were conquered by the Incas. From their capital in Cuzco, Peru, the Incas controlled an empire that included not only present-day Peru but Ecuador, parts of Argentina, and Chile. The empire was knitted together by a series of roads that were built across the Atacama Desert and through the Andes, as well as bridges that crossed treacherous ravines and deep valleys. The Incas mined rich deposits of gold and silver that provided a major source of their wealth. They also developed a highly sophisticated form of terrace agriculture. They built their farms and planted their crops along steep hillsides on the slopes of the Andes.

THE ARRIVAL OF THE SPANISH

Rumors of Incan wealth had reached the Spanish *conquistadors* who began arriving in the New World with Christopher Columbus in 1492. The Spanish conquered the Caribbean islands and, during the 1520s, took control of the rich Aztec Indian empire in Mexico. A decade later, a conquistador named Francisco Pizarro led a small army against the Incas in Peru. Pizarro and his men had heard rumors of the Incas' wealth and hoped to enrich themselves with treasures of gold and silver. Although Pizarro was greatly outnumbered, his men possessed superior weapons. These included guns, horses, and metal armor, which the Incas did not possess. Also, a civil war was raging among the Incas between two men who claimed the throne.

As a result, Pizarro's conquistadores defeated the Incas, executed their leaders, and took possession of their gold and silver treasures. In 1535, Pizarro founded a city, Lima, on the Peruvian coast, which became the capital of the Spanish empire in South America. About the same time, one of Pizarro's soldiers, Diego de Almagro, led an expedition southward into Chile. Almagro was hoping to find additional gold and silver. He was disappointed, however, and went back to Peru in 1537.

In 1540, another expedition headed south, led by the conquistador Pedro de Valdivia. According to *A History of Chile, 1808–1994* by Simon Collier and William Sater, upon first seeing the fertile central valley, Valdivia wrote, "This land is such that for living in, and for settling, there is none better in the world." The Spanish began to conquer the Indians living in the area. In 1541, Valdivia established a Spanish settlement at Santiago. Located on the Mapocho River in the fertile Chilean valley, Santiago became the capital of the new colony. The Spaniards faced resistance from the Mapuche, under their courageous chief Lautaro. War broke out with the Mapuche, who destroyed a Spanish fort and killed Valdivia. The Spanish sought their revenge, however, and eventually killed Lautaro at the Battle of Mataquito in 1557. Nevertheless, the war with the Mapuche continued, and the Spanish were unable to drive the Indians out of the lands south of the Bío-Bío River in southern Chile. The Mapuche continued to occupy these lands and prevent Spanish conquest for centuries.

THE SPANISH COLONY

Meanwhile, in other parts of the colony, the Spanish began to build towns. In addition to Santiago, the Spanish settled La Serena, north of the capital, beginning in 1543. They also established a settlement at Concepción, near the Bío-Bío in 1550, and at Valparaíso along the Pacific coast. Spanish governors gave large parcels of land to conquistadores who had participated in the conquest. These estates were known as *haciendas*. Each hacienda owner received an *encomienda*—a group of Indians assigned to work the land in return for food and a small amount of pay. In addition, the hacienda owners were supposed to convert the Indians to the Catholic religion.

The Spanish had brought Catholicism with them from Europe. During the eighth century, Spain had been conquered by Muslims. The Catholic kings of Spain were driven northward to a small area of the Spanish peninsula. Over the next seven centuries, however, the Catholics gradually reconquered Spain. The Muslims were driven out in 1492.

As a result of this experience, the Spanish had developed a strong, militant brand of Catholicism. They felt it was their duty to convert the people they conquered, such as the Indians in Chile, to Christianity. In reality, the Indians received little or nothing from the hacienda owners. There were relatively few conversions, and the Indians were treated almost as slaves. Meanwhile, thousands of Indians were stricken with diseases brought by the Spanish from Europe. Although the conquistadores had developed the ability to ward off diseases such as smallpox, the Indians' immune systems had not been exposed to these illnesses. As a result, many of them died.

Those who remained alive worked long hours on the Spanish haciendas in the fertile central valley of Chile. Hacienda owners grew wheat, cultivated grape vineyards for wine, and raised large herds of cattle. The cattle were slaughtered for beef and their hides were used to make leather shoes. Their fat was turned into tallow for making candles and soap. Part of the

PEDRO DE VALDIBIA.

Spanish conquistador Pedro de Valdivia *(above)* led an expedition in Chile in 1540. In 1541, de Valdivia established a settlement at Santiago, which today is Chile's capital city. Valdivia was killed during a war between the Spanish and the indigenous people of Chile, the Mapuche.

A LOVE OF ROAMING THE WORLD IS SOMETIMES TAKEN TO BE A DISTINCTIVE ASPECT OF THE CHILEAN NATIONAL CHARACTER

produce from the haciendas was sent north to Lima. According to *A History of Chile, 1808–1994,* one governor of Peru wrote that "Without Chile, [and its wheat], Lima would not exist."

Many of the hacienda owners and wealthy traders were *peninsulares.* These were Spaniards who had immigrated to Chile from the Spanish peninsula in Europe. They were considered the aristocrats of Chile, and some of them received noble titles from the Spanish government. Spain also prevented any settlers but the peninsulares from holding high offices in the colonial administration. In addition, they could not become Catholic bishops—leaders of the church in Chile.

A step below the peninsulares was another group of settlers, called the Creoles. Born in Chile, these were the children and grandchildren of Spanish parents. Some of the Creoles became prosperous estate owners. Others were traders or owned mines. These mines were in the Atacama Desert, where the Spanish had discovered gold and silver.

In addition to the peninsulares and Creoles, there was a large group of *mestizos.* They were the offspring of marriages between the Spanish conquistadores and the Indians in Chile. Some of the mestizos farmed small plots of land on the haciendas in return for herding cattle or carrying out other duties for the *haciendados,* or Spanish land owners. Others worked as migrant farmers, or *peóns,* moving from town to town. As historians Simon Collier and William Sater have written in *A History of Chile, 1808–1994,* "A love of roaming the world is sometimes taken to be a distinctive aspect of the Chilean national character. If so, its root may well lie here. Those peóns who drifted into casual labor in the towns became known as *rotos* ('ragged men'), a term later applied to the urban lower class as a whole."

In addition to these social classes, Chile maintained an army of about 1,500 soldiers during the eighteenth century. The soldiers were primarily used to guard the frontier south of the Bío-Bío. The commanding officers were generally members of the peninsulares.

GROWTH OF THE COLONY

Chile was far removed from Spain, so few immigrants arrived, and the colony did not grow very large. Settlers also may have avoided the colony because it was regularly struck by earthquakes. A severe quake, for example, destroyed much of Santiago in 1647. As a result, most homes in the colony were small and built of *adobe*, or bricks. It seemed to make little sense to the colonists to build elaborate houses when they could easily be destroyed by an earthquake.

Towns in Chile remained small, with a limited number of colonists. According to *A History of Chile, 1808–1994*, by the end of the eighteenth century, Valparaíso was described as "a small cluster of houses and ramshackle warehouses on an untidy beach." There were only about 4,000 residents. Santiago, the capital, was larger, with about 30,000 inhabitants. Many of the well-to-do hacienda owners spent part of the year in the capital and the rest of the time on their estates. The wealthy gave dances and dinners at their homes, providing the major form of social life and entertainment in the capital. By the beginning of the nineteenth century, Santiago also had a theater where well-to-do settlers, dressed in the latest and most expensive fashions, went to watch plays.

As the capital, Santiago was the location of the Spanish government. The administration included a governor appointed from Spain and an *audiencia*. This was a group of judges who tried cases and assisted the governor in running the colony.

Members of the audiencia were appointed from the ruling group, the peninsulares. Each town also had its own local government, called a *cabildo*. Members of the cabildo, called *regidores* (councilors) were appointed from among the well-to-do, including Creoles. These men purchased their positions on the cabildo. This money provided an important form of revenue for the colonial government, which also levied taxes on trade in and out of the colony.

THE COMING OF INDEPENDENCE

At the beginning of the nineteenth century, Spain controlled a vast empire in the New World. Spanish territory included much of the North American Southwest, Central America, islands in the Caribbean, and most of South America. The government was run by the Spanish king and the colonial governors who demanded strict obedience to the laws of Spain. Colonies like Chile were required to trade only with Spain or other parts of the Spanish empire. While a few traders and landowners possessed most of the wealth in the colony, the majority of settlers remained poor.

Change, however, had already begun to appear on the horizon. Several decades earlier, the United States had become independent of Great Britain as a result of the American Revolution. During the 1790s, the French overthrew and executed their monarch, Louis XVI, and became a republic. Under the leadership of General Napoleon Bonaparte, French armies streamed across Europe, conquering many established states. Finally, in 1808, Napoleon's armies invaded Spain, driving out the Spanish monarch Ferdinand VII.

Napoleon placed his brother, Joseph Bonaparte, on the Spanish throne. News of events in Spain crossed the Atlantic Ocean and created a major stir among the Spanish colonies in Latin America. In Chile, there had been a strong sense of loyalty to the Spanish crown. Peninsulares served in the colonial government. Creoles had received noble titles from the monarchy and felt an allegiance to the Spanish throne. Nevertheless, among some Creoles there had also been discontent. Chile had remained a relatively poor colony with a small population. Most trade had been funneled through Lima instead of Chilean ports, reducing the amount of money that could be made by Creole merchants. In addition, Creoles had been barred from high office.

As a result, the overthrow of the Spanish monarchy created a dilemma among the leaders of Chile. At first they continued to support Ferdinand VII and refused to recognize the new king. As time went on, however, the French continued to control the government, and Ferdinand showed no signs of having the military strength to regain his throne. Therefore, many Creoles believed that the time had come to create a new administration in Chile. In Santiago, the cabildo called leading members of the community to an assembly to consider what steps should be taken for the colony's future. The meeting began on September 18, 1810. During the gathering of political leaders, many of them called for a *junta*—a new government—to take control of the colony. September 18 became a national holiday in Chile, marking the beginning of the nation's independence movement.

Soon after its establishment, the junta raised a small army to defend the new government. Elsewhere in Latin America, uprisings had already begun against the Spanish colonial government. Clashes had occurred between colonists supporting independence and royalists who supported the existing Spanish empire. In Chile, a battle broke out in the spring of 1811 that led to the defeat of a royalist attempt to overthrow the junta. Later that year, the junta fell under the control of a successful military officer, José Miguel Carrera. Carrera called for important reforms in Chile. The colony's first newspaper was published, supporting the new government. In addition, in 1812, Carrera and the junta unveiled a new Chilean flag, which was yellow, blue, and white.

In Peru, the center of colonial government, the viceroy—or governor—Jose Fernando Abascal opposed the junta in Chile. Abascal raised an army and launched an invasion that he hoped would overthrow Carrera. In April 1813, Abascal's forces defeated Carrera. Early the following year, members of the junta decided to replace Carrera with a new military leader, Bernardo O'Higgins. A veteran of the battles against Abascal's troops, O'Higgins was a member of a distinguished Chilean family.

Carrera refused to recognize O'Higgins as the new leader of the junta forces. In fact, Carrera led a coup that toppled the junta in 1814 and took control of the government. Meanwhile, Spanish forces were advancing on Santiago to retake Chile and restore it to the empire. In October 1814, Carrera and O'Higgins—commanding separate armies—were defeated by the royalists and forced to flee to Argentina. There they joined the army of José de San Martín, who was leading the fight for Argentine independence against Spain.

By this time, Napoleon had been defeated in Europe and Ferdinand VII had returned as king of Spain. King Ferdinand spearheaded the effort by Spanish troops to retake the colonies in South America. At first, the king's effort to restore his empire met with success. In Chile, for example, some independence leaders were sent into exile, while others were brutally murdered. Instead of putting an end to the revolt, however, these actions simply convinced many Chileans to continue fighting. Guerrilla forces harassed the Spanish troops with hit-and-run tactics over the next three years.

During the winter of 1817, San Martín, along with Chilean troops commanded by O'Higgins, made a difficult march across the icy Andes into Chile. In February, they met royalist forces at the Battle of Chacabuco, where O'Higgins led a cavalry charge that sealed a hard-fought victory against royalist troops. As a result, O'Higgins and San Martín led a victorious march into Santiago, where they were welcomed by cheering

The above image depicts the 1818 Battle of Maipo, which resulted in the independence of Chile from Spanish rule. The war was fought between Spanish royalists and South American troops led by General San Martín, who secured the Chilean victory.

crowds. In 1818, O'Higgins announced that Chile had become an independent republic.

While O'Higgins may have believed that the war was over, the royalists were not finished. Their armies still operated in other parts of Chile. Early in 1818, they inflicted a major defeat

"CHILE WILL NEVER FORGET THE NAME OF THE ILLUSTRIOUS INVALID WHO, TODAY, PRESENTED HIMSELF ON THE BATTLEFIELD!"

—San Martín

on O'Higgins, who received severe wounds during the battle. Nevertheless, San Martín gathered the remaining Chilean and Argentine forces together and defeated the royalists at Maipo, near Santiago, on April 5, 1818. As historians Collier and Sater wrote in *A History of Chile, 1808–1994*, "Believing the . . . [battle] to be still in doubt, the wounded O'Higgins galloped onto the scene with reinforcements. 'Glory to the savior of Chile!' he exclaimed, embracing San Martín. Overcome with emotion, the great Argentine replied: 'Chile will never forget the name of the illustrious invalid who, today, presented himself on the battlefield!' Such was the 'embrace of Maipo,' never to be forgotten by Chileans."

O'Higgins replaced Chile's first flag with a new one. The new flag is red and white, with a blue square in the corner and a white star inside the square, and is still the national flag of Chile today.

3

The Growth of Independent Chile

DURING MOST OF THE CENTURY AND A HALF AFTER INDEPENDENCE, CHILE was a democracy. The president and the Congress were elected by the people. From time to time, however, conflicts broke out that interrupted the smooth flow of democratic government. Sometimes these conflicts occurred between the Congress and the president. In addition, great inequalities existed within Chilean society between the small number of wealthy citizens and the vast majority of poor peóns. As a result, strikes and protests broke out as the poor tried to claim what they thought was rightfully theirs. To deal with the unrest, the Chilean military periodically stepped in, overthrew the Chilean democracy, and took control of the government.

THE NEW GOVERNMENT

As the liberator of Chile from Spanish rule, Bernardo O'Higgins seemed the natural choice to become the leader of the new, independent republic. He was widely supported by the majority of Chileans who were grateful for everything that he had done to achieve independence. The new leader, who called himself the supreme director, believed that Chile needed a period of peace and stability after the turmoil of the civil war. As historian Guillermo I. Castillo-Feliú wrote in *Culture and Customs of Chile*, "It is indisputable that O'Higgins's government was a dictatorship." As O'Higgins once put it, according to *A History of Chile, 1808–1994*, if Chileans "will not become happy by their own efforts, they shall be made happy by force. By God! They *shall* be happy."

O'Higgins surrounded himself with a few close friends who helped him run the republic. He did not establish an elected legislature, although Chileans wanted it. Many of the Creoles who had hoped to take power in the new government were disappointed. In addition, O'Higgins angered other members of the Chilean elite when he eliminated noble titles. The well-to-do colonists who had been awarded these titles in the past by the Spanish government regarded them as symbols of their high status in Chile. O'Higgins also gave Chilean military support to General San Martín in his efforts to liberate Peru. O'Higgins recognized that an independent Peru would protect Chile's northern border. Many Chileans criticized him, however, for wasting their nation's resources on the Peruvian fight for independence. As a result of all these issues, O'Higgins was driven from office by a junta in 1823 and never returned to Chile.

SUCCESSORS OF O'HIGGINS

O'Higgins was succeeded by Ramón Freire, who had led the junta that had overthrown Chile's former political leader. Freire governed with a Chilean Congress that was elected by the well-to-do citizens of the country. During much of the decade, however, a debate raged over the direction of the government. Chilean Liberals wanted a strong Congress to restrict the powers of the president, while Conservatives wanted a strong president. Ramón Freire was followed by a Liberal, Francisco Antonio Pinto. But in 1830, the Conservatives staged a revolt against Pinto. They gathered an army, under the leadership of General Joaquin Prieto, and drove Pinto from office.

General Prieto served as president for the next decade, governing a nation of about one million residents. But the most powerful man in the government was a member of the president's cabinet, Diego Portales. Diego Portales was born in Santiago, the son of a well-to-do Chilean family. In his 20s, he became a successful merchant and traveled to Peru to improve his business. According to "Diego Portales: A Chilean Biography" by Charlene Richardson (posted on Historicaltextarchive.com), Portales—a keen observer of South American politics—wrote that "a strong government" was necessary to run a nation, led by men who were "true models of virtue and patriotism," who could lead citizens "on the road of order and virtues. When they have made themselves moral," Portales said, "the government comes to be completely liberal, free and full of ideals, where all citizens take part."

Portales returned to Chile during the 1820s and bought a newspaper in Valparaíso. Meanwhile, he had been developing contacts with many influential politicians. When some of his allies won the elections in 1828, Portales joined the new government as minister of the interior.

Under the leadership of the 37-year-old Portales, the Conservatives called a convention and wrote a new constitution in 1833. This constitution gave wide powers to the president of the Republic. He could be elected, and then reelected for two five-year terms. In addition, he had the power to suspend basic freedoms—like freedom of the press—during an emergency when the government seemed threatened. Called a state of siege, it enabled the president to rule as a dictator without any checks from the Chilean Congress. The new constitution restricted voting primarily to men who were literate and owned property. As a result, only a relatively small number of voters determined congressional and presidential elections. A majority of these voters were controlled by Portales.

Portales never ran for president. As historians Simon Collier and William Sater wrote in *A History of Chile, 1808–1994*, "He could have had the presidency for the asking, but never asked. This in itself could well have helped to inhibit [prevent] the development of a caudillo tradition in Chile." The tradition of the *caudillo*, or dictator who remained in power indefinitely, occurred in many other South American countries. Chile was one of the exceptions.

There are other reasons why Chile may have avoided the caudillo tradition. Other nations in Latin America had a large slave population. In Chile, however, there were only 4,000 slaves, who had been freed by O'Higgins. As a result, according to the U.S. Department of the Army's *Chile: A Country Study*, "the Chilean elite was less fearful than many other Spanish Americans that . . . democracy would open the door to uprisings by massive native or black subject classes." The elite also felt confident of staying in power in a democracy. They controlled the land and the successful trading businesses.

Through his influence, Portales largely controlled the politicians who served in the cabinet and ran for office in Congress. As one of his opponents put it, according to *A History of Chile, 1808–1994*, "Portales has got a million people in his pocket." Portales and his associates did not hesitate to bribe voters and even arrest those who might vote against their supporters at election time.

Meanwhile, during the 1830s, the Chilean economy flourished under Portales's leadership. New silver mines were discovered in the northern part of Chile around Copiapó. Copper mining expanded, and Chilean wheat continued to be exported abroad.

Diego Portales *(above)*, a Chilean politician, was an extremely powerful member of General Prieto's presidential cabinet. Portales greatly influenced the creation of the Chilean Constitution of 1833 and also helped lead Chile into war with Peru. In 1837, Portales was assassinated by Chileans who were opposed to the war.

Less than 1,000 rich hacienda owners controlled almost 70 percent of the land.

Across the border in Peru, however, tensions began to mount against the Chilean government. Peru imposed a tariff on Chilean wheat, hurting its export trade. In retaliation, Chile imposed a high tariff on sugar coming from Peru, hurting the Peruvian economy. As tensions increased, war loomed between the countries. To strengthen its position for the coming conflict, Peru formed an alliance with Bolivia, located on the Chilean border.

War broke out in 1836, although many Chileans did not support it. (Portales was captured by a Chilean colonel and his soldiers who were opposed to the conflict and on June 6, 1837, was assassinated by more than 30 thrusts from their bayonets.) Nevertheless, under the leadership of General Manuel Bulnes, the Chilean army was victorious, bringing an end to the conflict by 1839. In 1841, Bulnes was elected president of Chile.

GROWTH OF THE REPUBLIC

During the next three decades, the Chilean economy continued to grow. By the 1870s, as much as one half of the world's copper was being mined in Chile. Copper played a key role as a raw material in the production of electrical wire and manufacturing equipment. A railroad line that began operating during the 1850s linked Chilean mining centers. Coal mining also began to develop in the southern part of Chile, providing an important source of fuel. Nevertheless, about 80 percent of the Chilean population still worked in agriculture. Most of them were employed on large haciendas, growing wheat and barley, tending grape vineyards, and herding sheep and beef. Less than 1,000 hacienda owners controlled almost 70 percent of the land.

These wealthy haciendados enjoyed a large worldwide market for their products. During the 1850s, for example, a gold rush was underway in California. Wheat and flour were exported from Chile to feed the California miners. In Chile, which lies in the Southern Hemisphere, the seasons are reversed from the Northern Hemisphere. When it was winter in Europe and North America, Chilean wheat was being harvested during the summer in the Southern Hemisphere. As a result, there was a huge demand for Chilean wheat in North America, England, and other European countries.

The Chilean port of Valparaíso was filled with ships carrying exports to North America and Europe. By the 1860s, Valparaíso was linked to Santiago by a railroad line. Valparaíso's population, which had reached 100,000 by 1875, constructed a theater, opened newspapers, and lit the streets with fashionable gas lamps. Chile's other major city, the capital Santiago, also expanded, with the population reaching 150,000 by the 1870s. The city laid out new roads and constructed a public park. Meanwhile, the well-to-do built magnificent homes in the city center to show off their wealth. Nevertheless, the majority of the city's inhabitants remained poor. On the outskirts of Santiago, they lived in poor *barrios* (neighborhoods), with families crowded into run-down *ranchos* (shacks). The city's water was polluted, which allowed disease to become rampant. Many people died of typhoid, an infection carried by contaminated water, or they were stricken by tuberculosis, a disease of the lungs.

THE WAR OF THE PACIFIC

The strong power of the president finally led to a reaction during the 1860s and 1870s. A majority of newly elected congressmen passed laws to limit the power of the president and increase the role of Congress in the government. For example, presidents were no longer permitted to serve two back-to-back five-year terms in office.

In 1879 Chile fought against the joint forces of Bolivia and Peru in what is now known as the War of the Pacific. Chile came out victorious. It gained control of nitrate and copper-rich areas around Antofagasta, and also won control of Tarapacá; two areas that were originally Peruvian territory.

In 1876, a liberal political leader, Aníbal Pinto, was elected president. During much of his presidency, Pinto was involved in a new war with Peru and Bolivia. The war began in Antofagasta, which was then part of Bolivia. Chilean companies had earlier been given the right by the Bolivian government to mine nitrates in the area. Nitrates were a rich source of fertilizer in agriculture, and, therefore, in great demand throughout much of the world. In 1878, the Bolivian government decided to increase the taxes it charged Chilean companies to do business around Antofagasta.

Under pressure from voters, President Pinto sent the Chilean army into Bolivia and captured Antofagasta. In 1879, Bolivia and Peru declared war on Chile—a conflict known as the War of the Pacific. The Chilean army and navy were much smaller than the combined forces of Peru and Bolivia. Nevertheless in 1879, the Chilean navy won a major victory over Peruvian battleships and took control of the Pacific coast. Following this victory, the Chilean army invaded Peru and captured the capital, Lima, early in 1881. After a guerrilla war in Peru that continued until 1883, Chile eventually signed a peace treaty with Peru; and, in 1884, with Bolivia. As a result of the war, rich nitrate and copper areas around Antofagasta as well as Tarapacá (which had belonged to Peru) became part of Chile. As historian Guillermo I. Castillo-Feliú wrote in *Culture and Customs of Chile*, "The war proved to be an economic bonanza for Chile."

TOPPLING A PRESIDENT

Winning a war had increased the prestige and the power of the Chilean president. Nevertheless, many members of Congress believed that the president had become too powerful. They pointed to efforts by the president to control elections with bribes and even violence. As one observer reported about the presidential election of 1885, according to *A History of Chile, 1808–1994*, there was "a good deal of disorder and not a little loss of life, revolvers, knives and stones having been freely used. At one [voting] table, six people were killed and thirty wounded." As a result of the election José Balmaceda, age 46, was elected president. A liberal, Balmaceda had served as minister of the interior.

Soon after entering office, President Balmaceda began a large program of public works. These projects included building schools, improving the country's railroad system, and constructing a bridge over the Bío-Bío River. Some Conservative congressmen, however, were opposed to spending money on these projects, believing that they were too expensive. In addition, President Balmaceda had to deal with changes in the nitrates industry. Gradually, foreign investors had begun to buy up the nitrate fields and threatened to take control of them. Foreign control might threaten Chilean independence as well as the livelihoods of the local nitrate owners.

Political opposition, consisting of Conservatives as well as the Chilean nitrate owners, began to gather against President Balmaceda. Meanwhile, strikes were breaking out across Chile, led by men who wanted better working conditions in the mines and the nitrate fields. Congress and the president refused to work together to run the government and deal with the strikes. When President Balmaceda decided to govern without Congress, a majority of the congressmen voted to remove him from office.

In 1891, a civil war broke out between military forces loyal to the president and those supporting Congress. By late summer, President Balmaceda's forces had been defeated. Following his defeat, the president committed suicide.

A NEW BRAND OF POLITICS

As a result of the civil war, the powerful Chilean president was replaced by what was called a Parliamentary Republic, lasting from 1891 until 1925. The new president, Jorge Montt, was the leader of the congressional and military leaders who had overthrown the president. While in the past the president had selected his cabinet ministers, Congress now selected the members of the president's cabinet. Nevertheless, other aspects of the electoral system did not change. Congressmen did not hesitate to bribe voters in order to win their seats, and elections were still marred by violence.

Meanwhile, economic changes were occurring across Chile. Manufacturing was growing in the cities. Thousands of peóns were leaving the countryside to move to Santiago, Valparaíso and other cities, hoping for better jobs. Wages, however, were

WHILE A FEW CHILEANS CONTINUED TO GROW RICH, THE VAST MAJORITY REMAINED POOR.

low among factory workers, miners, and dock workers. As a result, many of them began joining unions, which demanded higher wages and better working conditions for their members. Strikes broke out at mines and factories as union members refused to work unless their demands were met. In December 1907, nitrate workers staged a huge strike in northern Chile. The government responded by calling in the military to force the strikers back to work. Hundreds of workers were killed before the strike finally ended.

Two years later, a national confederation of various labor groups was formed, calling itself Federación de Obreros de Chile, FOCH, the Federation of Chilean Workers. New political parties also arose to represent the interests of these workers. These parties included the Democratic Party and the Socialists. The Socialists wanted to create greater equality between the rich and poor. Their programs included a government take over of major industries, like copper mining, to increase revenues and provide more jobs and income for Chile's peóns.

Many Chileans supported FOCH, the Democratic Party, or the Socialists because of the economic conditions inside the country. While a few Chileans continued to grow rich, the vast majority remained poor. The copper mines and the nitrate fields were being dominated by foreign-owned companies. The Chilean government taxed these companies heavily. Nevertheless, they took their profits out of Chile, which angered many Chileans.

CHILE AND WORLD WAR I

Meanwhile, the Chilean economy began to decline as a result of events across the Atlantic Ocean. In 1914, World War I

Chile's economy took a down turn after the nation's civil war. At the dawn of the twentieth century, most Chileans were impoverished. This 1900 photograph shows squalid conditions on Chilean streets.

broke out in Europe. The Allies—Great Britain, France and Russia—faced the Central Powers—Germany and Austria-Hungary—in a brutal war that lasted for the next four years. Chile remained neutral during the war. Chilean exports, however, especially nitrates, were cut off by naval blockades established by each side to starve the other side into surrendering. Just before the war had begun, Germany had also started to produce artificially made nitrates. These were used for agriculture and as a major ingredient in gunpowder. Over the next decade, artificial nitrates would lead to a major decline in the Chilean nitrate business.

THE ALESSANDRI GOVERNMENT

After World War I ended in 1918, much of Europe and the United States slipped into a major recession. This further worsened economic conditions inside Chile. Massive strikes and demonstrations broke out, as workers demanded that the government make new efforts to improve the lives of the poor. A political group formed calling itself the Liberal Alliance. The Liberal Alliance was made up of Liberals, Democrats and Radicals. The Radicals were a relatively new party that represented middle-class voters. The Alliance nominated a member of Congress—Arturo Alessandri—as their candidate for president in 1920. Alessandri was a gifted speaker. As historians Simon Collier and William Slater wrote in *A History of Chile, 1808–1994,* "He was the nearest any modern Chilean politician has ever come to being a 'charismatic leader.' He could hold a crowd as few others have been able to do." Alessandri promised reforms that would improve the working conditions of the poor. He was strongly opposed, however, by the well-to-do and the middle classes, who feared that he might create turmoil in the economy. The vote in the presidential election was close, but Alessandri was narrowly elected.

President Alessandri soon discovered that being elected and running the country were completely different. As the president tried to initiate his reforms, he was opposed by a majority of the Congress. Since neither side was willing to compromise, nothing was accomplished. Meanwhile, a group of young military officers was becoming frustrated with the political deadlock. They recognized the need for reforms to help the poor. In addition, they were fearful that the deadlock might prevent Congress from spending money to maintain the armed forces. When the deadlock continued, the young officers threatened to use force if Congress did not act.

New laws were finally passed in 1924. In reaction, a group of Conservative officers led a military coup that ousted Alessandri in September. But they ruled for only a short time before they were driven out by officers loyal to Alessandri. Among them was Colonel Carlos Ibáñez del Campo, who served as minister of war. Chile's military rulers enacted a new constitution in 1925. This constitution changed the presidential term of office from five years to six years, and increased the powers of the president. In addition, the constitution made a commitment to safeguard the welfare of all Chileans—rich as well as poor.

CHILE AND THE GREAT DEPRESSION

Alessandri left the presidency at the end of 1925. In 1927, one of the leaders of the military coup, Carlos Ibáñez, was elected president. He had previously served as vice president of Chile. According to the U.S. Department of the Army's *Chile: A Country Study,* he "based his reign on military support (especially from the army), [and] on repression (especially of labor unions). . . . He also created the national police, known as the Carabineros." The police helped him control the country as a virtual dictator. Ibáñez began a vast program of public works, financed in part by huge loans from U.S. banks, while also making improvements in the military, such as adding ships to the Chilean navy.

His administration, however, was also forced to deal with an economic crisis. In 1930, the Great Depression began to engulf the economies of nations around the world. Loans from the United States dried up. Prices for copper and nitrate fell rapidly, throwing 25 percent of Chileans out of work. Protests broke out on the streets of Santiago and other cities, as workers demanded

General Carlos Ibáñez del Campo was elected president of Chile in 1927. While serving as president, Ibáñez created a Chilean national police force called the Carabineros and made improvements to the country's military. In this 1930 photograph, Chilean soldiers train and exercise.

that the government take action to help the unemployed. The police stepped in, killing some of the demonstrators. While the Chilean people hoped for new economic programs from the government, Ibáñez and his closest advisers were unable to deal with the economic catastrophe. In July 1931, the president resigned from office and left Chile to live in Argentina.

What followed in Chile was a year and a half of instability. When political leaders proved unable to improve economic conditions, military leaders staged a coup and took over the government in 1932. Calling their administration the Socialist Republic, they promised to take over the major industries—such as copper mining—and put people back to work. Chileans, however, did not believe that Socialism was the solution to their economic problems. As a result, the military leaders called for new elections late in 1932. The presidential race brought victory to Arturo Alessandri, who had served as president during the 1920s. He returned to the presidency, hoping to lead his country out of the economic crisis.

POLITICAL STABILITY

In Alessandri's second term as president, the Chilean economic situation began to improve. During the 1930s, the world economy gradually started to make a comeback from the economic depression. There was greater demand for Chile's copper. The government raised taxes on foreign-owned copper companies, providing more money to promote public works programs that would employ workers. Tariffs on foreign imports were raised, making them more costly than locally produced products. As a result, Chilean production began to increase and Chilean workers in the cities gradually found new employment. Meanwhile, farm production increased to meet the growing demands of city workers. The government also controlled prices on food so poor workers could afford to buy enough to eat.

While Alessandri's measures helped improve the economy, some Chilean politicians wanted him to go even further. In 1936, a new political party, called the Popular Front, was formed by the Radicals, the Socialists, and the Communists. The Communist Party had risen to power in Russia during a revolution in 1918. During the revolution, the autocratic Russian czar was overthrown and later executed. In Russia, renamed the Soviet Union, the Communists took control of

MORE THAN 75 PERCENT OF ALL CHILEANS WERE EITHER UNDERNOUR- ISHED OR SERIOUSLY MALNOURISHED

the economy and promised jobs to millions of workers who had remained poor during the czarist regime. The Soviet experiment inspired political leaders in countries across the world, where Communist parties began to arise. In 1922, the Communist Party of Chile was founded. Communists and Socialists became leaders of Chile's labor unions, staging strikes and demanding higher wages for workers.

In the 1930s, Chile still had deep inequalities between its social classes. According to *A History of Chile, 1808–1994*, an international study completed in the 1930s revealed that "more than 75 percent of all Chileans were either undernourished or seriously malnourished." Many voters supported the programs of the Popular Front, which were aimed at improving the lives of the poor.

PRESIDENTS IN THE 1930s AND 1940s
In 1938, the Popular Front won the presidential election, and its leader Pedro Cerda became president of the Chilean repub-lic. Cerda served only three years of a six-year term before dying in office. Under Popular Front leadership, however, the number of unions in Chile increased. The Popular Front also formed the Production Development Corporation, providing loans to new manufacturing businesses. Cerda was succeeded by two other presidents who won with the support of Socialists, Communists, and Radicals. Juan Ríos governed Chile until 1946, when he was succeeded by Gabriel Videla, who served as president from 1946 to 1952.

By the late 1940s, the Cold War had broken out between the United States and the Soviet Union. Communist govern-ments had arisen throughout Eastern Europe, supported by troops from the Soviet Union. Inside Chile, Communists had increased their power in the trade unions, calling more strikes that disrupted Chilean industry. Violence broke out during a strike in Santiago. Violent strikes also occurred in the copper mines and the coal mines, forcing President Videla to call out the army to restore order. Finally, in 1948, Videla outlawed the Communist Party in Chile. The president's action pleased the United States, which had been providing economic assistance to Chile. Nevertheless, the Communists continued to work inside the unions, even organizing large street demonstrations against the government.

As unrest continued in Chile, the economy began to decline. Chilean governments spent more money than they received in the form of taxes. To deal with the deficits, the government printed money. With more and more money in circulation, Chilean currency was worth less and less. Prices rose as merchants hoped to make up for a decline in the value of currency by charging more money for their products. As a result, inflation gripped the country.

POLITICS IN THE 1950s

Many voters had become tired of Videla's leadership. In the 1952 presidential election they turned to a familiar politician, a former president who had resigned during the Great Depression—Carlos Ibáñez. As a campaign symbol, Ibáñez used a broom to indicate that he would make a clean sweep of Chile's past corrupt governments. Although Ibáñez tried to restore order in Chile, the strikes continued. With the support of the army, President Ibáñez suspended political freedoms, arrested union leaders, and declared a state of siege. Nevertheless, inflation continued, with living costs rising by almost 90 percent annually to create huge financial problems for most Chileans.

In 1958, voters went to the polls to elect a new president. Many of Ibáñez's supporters had grown tired of him and

Although a new leader had come to power, the same old problems remained.

formed a new political party, the Christian Democrats. The Christian Democrats wanted reforms that would improve working conditions and the lives of the rural peóns, but they were opposed to Socialism because it seemed too radical. The Christian Democrats nominated Eduardo Frei to run for president. The Socialists nominated Dr. Salvador Allende—who had also run for president against Ibáñez in 1952. A third nominee was Jorge Alessandri—son of a former president—who had served in the Popular Front cabinet during the late 1940s. Alessandri had been selected by an alliance of Liberal and Conservative political leaders. In a close election, Alessandri edged Allende to become president of Chile.

Although a new leader had come to power, the same old problems remained. Inflation continued and the government seemed powerless to stop it. To bring in more money, Alessandri increased taxes on the now-U.S.-owned copper mines. But the mining companies were paying so much that they had to raise the price of copper on the world market. This meant that it could not compete with lower-priced copper from other parts of the world. Although Alessandri reduced inflation for the first part of his presidential term, it once again began to increase during the last years of his presidency. Meanwhile, Alessandri made little effort to improve the lot of the rural poor, who wanted land redistribution and a breakup of the large haciendas.

The large gulf between rich and poor Chileans remained. Major events, however, were about to change the lives of the Chilean people.

The Bachelets and the Chilean Government

VERÓNICA MICHELLE BACHELET JERIA WAS BORN IN SANTIAGO, THE capital of Chile, on September 29, 1951. Her mother, Ángela Jeria Gómez, was an anthropologist, and her father, Alberto Bachelet Martínez, was an officer in the Chilean air force. During the period when the nation was struggling with economic problems, a military career was one of the most secure jobs in Chile.

BACHELET'S CHILDHOOD

In the early 1950s, when Michelle was still an infant, Gabriel Videla was completing his term as president of the republic. Chile was dealing with striking bus drivers in Santiago and massive strikes by miners in the copper mines. As a result of unsettled conditions across the country, voters decided to bring back General Carlos Ibáñez for a second term as president.

53

Ibáñez, however, also proved unable to deal with the strikes and finally declared a state of siege in 1954.

While Michelle was a child, her father was posted to various military bases around Chile. This meant that the family, including Michelle and her older brother, Alberto, were required to move often. Michelle attended four different elementary schools during her childhood. Among them were schools in San Bernardo and Quintero, located in central Chile, and Antofagasta in the north. In 1960, when Michelle was 8, an earthquake struck Chile. The military often worked with the government to rescue victims of quakes. During this relief operation, Michelle's father met Dr. Salvador Allende, who was also involved in the relief effort. According to a January 4, 2003, article in *The New York Times*, Allende "came to appreciate [his] organizational skills" in the operation.

LIVING IN THE UNITED STATES

In 1962, while Michelle was a child, her father was posted to the United States. He served in the Chilean embassy in Washington, D.C. The Bachelets found a home in Bethesda, Maryland, near Washington, where Michelle attended middle school. "It was hard for her in the beginning," her mother was quoted as saying in a January 16, 2006, article in *The New York Times*. "For the first three months, she cried when she came home from school, because she didn't understand any of what was being said." Michelle, however, soon learned to speak English. ". . . [A]fter six months she was fully integrated," her mother continued, "and so we were able to travel around and get to know the United States and Canada and visit places like Niagara Falls." Nevertheless, as noted in a January 25, 2006, report by PBS's Online News Hour, Michelle was struck by the fact "such a huge and powerful country knew so little about so many, many countries. . . . Nobody knew anything about Chile. . . . They thought we lived in, like, Indian houses, things like that."

This was a period of great turmoil in the United States. According to the January 16, 2006, *New York Times* article, "Friends and relatives recall that the pre-adolescent Ms. Bachelet was shocked by the racial segregation she saw in America and by the assassination of John F. Kennedy." President Kennedy was assassinated in November 1963, the year after Michelle's family came to the United States.

THE FREI GOVERNMENT

At the end of 1963, the Bachelet family returned to Chile, which was also struggling with political turmoil. Massive labor strikes had returned to the country, and many Chileans realized that major reforms were necessary before their nation would become more stable. Therefore, in 1964, Chilean voters elected Christian Democrat leader Eduardo Frei as president. Born in Santiago in 1911, Frei became a lawyer in 1933. After entering politics, he was elected to the Chilean Senate in 1949. During the 1950s, Frei and some of his associates founded the Christian Democratic Party. Defeated for president in 1958, he ran successfully in 1964. Frei had promised reforms in agriculture and industry. At first, his efforts were blocked by a Conservative congress. In 1965, however, the Christian Democratic Party won majorities in the congressional elections, enabling Frei to win approval for his reform program.

Some of these reforms were aimed at helping the urban poor who had flocked into cities like Santiago, looking for better lives. During Frei's term in office, the government built more than 250,000 new homes for city workers. In addition, Frei's administration expanded hospital services to treat the sick, and constructed 3,000 schools across the country. As a result, an estimated 95 percent of Chilean children were attending elementary school.

To assist the people who lived in the countryside, Frei encouraged the growth of rural unions. These represented the interests of agricultural workers, demanding higher wages and

In this 1964 photograph, Christian Democrat Eduardo Frei holds two fingers in the air to remind voters that his name is second on the ballot. Promising the Chilean people reforms in agriculture and industry, Frei won the vote and was elected president. In 1994, Frei's eldest son, Eduardo Frei-Ruiz Tagle followed in his father's footsteps and became president of Chile.

better working conditions. In addition, Frei began to redistribute land to Chilean peasants. Large farms were broken up, with the owners paid by the government and the land given over to poor farmers. Finally, Frei took control of 51 percent of the major American copper companies—Kennecott and Anaconda. Some American managers were replaced by Chilean executives. Meanwhile, the price of copper increased, bringing more income to the government.

Nevertheless, inflation continued to rise during the 1960s. Government expenditures on schools, hospitals, and land purchases exceeded income, fueling inflation. President Frei also had to deal with other problems. He was criticized by Conservatives for initiating too many reforms, jeopardizing the positions of rich haciendados in the countryside. On the left, Socialists and Communists criticized Frei for not going far enough to remake the Chilean economy.

The late 1960s was a period of worldwide protest. In the United States, students marched in the streets and on college campuses against the war in Vietnam. Protest songs by the Beatles and Bob Dylan became international best-sellers. In Chile, students were involved in political protests against the policies of the government. At the height of these protests, Michelle Bachelet was graduating from high school. Michelle was an outstanding student who had been elected president of her class. She had also been one of the originators of a popular band known as Las Clap Clap. A guitarist, Michelle played the songs of Bob Dylan and Joan Baez. In 1970, after an unusually high score on college admission exams, Michelle became a medical student at the University of Chile. As her cousin Alicia Galdames said in the January 16, 2006, *New York Times* article on Bachelet, "We were teenagers immersed in the political and social movements that were transforming Chile and the world. The seeds of her ideals were planted in this period."

THE ALLENDE GOVERNMENT

Those ideals were represented by a new government that came to office in Chile as a result of the presidential elections of 1970. Since Frei could not run for a second term as president, the Christian Democrats nominated Radomiro Tomic—another leader of the party. Jorge Alessandri, a former Chilean president, was the candidate of the National Party, representing the

Conservatives in Chile. On the left, the Socialists, Radicals, and Communists joined to form the Popular Unity Party (UP) and nominated Salvador Allende as their candidate. Allende wanted to push the reforms started by Frei even further. In a close vote, Allende was elected president.

Born in Valparaíso in 1908, Salvador Allende attended the University of Chile, where he received a medical degree in 1933. During the late 1930s, he was a founder of the Chilean Socialist Party and served in the government of Pedro Cerda as minister of health. In the 1940s, Allende was elected a senator in the Chilean Congress, and he ran for president in 1952, 1958, and 1964. Allende called himself a Marxist—a follower of Karl Marx, the nineteenth-century German philosopher who laid down the principles of Socialism and Communism.

The United States government was opposed to the election of Allende as president of Chile. U.S. leaders feared that under his administration, Chile might become an ally of the Soviet Union. During the election of 1970, the U.S. administration of President Richard Nixon supported Jorge Alessandri, hoping that he might defeat Allende. Nevertheless, Allende was elected with 36 percent of the vote to 35 percent for Alessandri. If no candidate obtained a majority, the Chilean constitution called for Congress to select the president—usually the candidate with the most votes. According to Lois Hecht Oppenheim's *Politics in Chile*, at the last minute, the U.S. Central Intelligence Agency worked behind the scenes to persuade the Congress to vote for Alessandri. The CIA also conspired with the military to overthrow the government. Neither plan worked, however, and Allende became president of Chile.

As Allende took office, Michelle Bachelet had become a member of the student wing of the Socialist Party. As one of her friends recalled in the January 16, 2006, *New York Times* article, "She was really studious, very disciplined and responsible and sure of herself, but with a tremendous capacity for empathy. It was a time of black and white, but she managed to get along with everybody, no matter what their political persuasion. She wasn't one to look for fights; on the contrary, she was the one who was tolerant, always looking for consensus [agreement]."

There was little agreement to be found in Chile, however, as President Allende began to initiate his reforms. Allende wanted to provide free milk for schoolchildren, day care centers for the poor, and health clinics. Over the next two years, total government spending on social programs almost doubled, although these measures were opposed by Conservatives.

Allende also proposed major changes in the Chilean economy. In 1971, Chile took complete control of the large copper companies—the so-called Gran Minería del Cobre. This measure had wide support in the Chilean Congress. The government and most other elected officials were convinced that this decision would lead to greater revenues and higher employment for Chilean workers. Immediately after nationalization, the government hired more miners. Many of them were unskilled, however, and production declined. In addition, there was no money to substantially increase the wages for the miners. This led to massive strikes in the copper mines, reducing production further and driving down revenues for the government. Meanwhile, worldwide copper prices were falling.

Early in his administration, Allende established diplomatic relations with the Communist government of Cuba, led by Fidel Castro. This angered the United States and nations in Latin America that had cut off relations with the Castro government. Castro visited Chile, where he traveled the country with Allende and addressed huge gatherings. Conservatives, however, feared that Allende might turn Chile into a Communist state like Cuba.

PROBLEMS FOR ALLENDE

Conservatives pointed to Chilean industry, where the Allende administration nationalized many factories. Some of these were large plants owned by American manufacturers such as

After unsuccessfully running for president in 1952, 1958, and 1962, Salvador Allende narrowly won the election in 1970. In 1973, his presidency was cut short when General Augusto Pinochet led a coup d'état and seized power of Chile. In the photograph above, Allende and his wife, Hortensia Bussi de Allende pose on their balcony the day after he won the presidential election.

Ford. U.S. managers were replaced by government appointees, who were often not as skilled in running the plants. Additional employees were hired to provide more jobs. This, however, only added to manufacturing costs, while inefficiency led to a fall in production.

In the countryside, Allende continued to break up large land holdings. This process had begun under President Frei, but Allende went much further. According to Oppenheim's *Politics in Chile*, by mid-1972, the government had taken control of more than 4,600 large farms—almost three times the number broken up by Frei. Much of the land was taken over by the Chilean government and the farmers became employees of the state. Many peasants, however, did not want to work for the government. They wanted to become independent farmers. There were protests among the peasants, which helped reduce the size of harvests. Small farmers also feared that their lands might be taken by the government, so they refused to harvest any crops. As a result, food supplies necessary to feed city workers began to decline.

The rest of the economy was not doing much better. Not only had the government increased expenditures on social programs, it also began to increase workers' wages. Meanwhile, the Nixon administration was using its influence with international banks to ensure that Chile did not receive any loans to finance its programs. According to *Politics in Chile*, as President Nixon put it, he wanted to "make the Chilean economy scream." The Chilean government tried to deal with the situation by issuing more money. This only drove up inflation.

In the meantime, protests broke out over the shortage of food. In December 1971, crowds of women joined the "March of the Empty Saucepans" to complain about the worsening food situation. Violent strikes erupted in many parts of the country. One of these, a strike by truckers that broke out in October 1972, lasted more than three weeks. The strike was a response to the government's policy of taking over a few private trucking businesses. Other independent truckers feared that they might be next. In sympathy, many store owners closed their doors. Others, including doctors and lawyers, joined the strike, which was supported by the National Party and the Christian Democratic Party. Both political groups were opposed to the

Unrest grew across the nation as inflation increased to more than 500 percent annually and food shortages multiplied.

Allende administration. According to Oppenheim's *Politics in Chile*, the strike was also assisted by money from the CIA, which hoped to create instability in Chile and weaken the Allende government.

According to Oppenheim, "The strike's effect on daily life was dramatic. Chile is an extremely long, narrow country, and most goods are transported by truck. . . . Goods from outlying areas, or from the port at Valparaíso, could not get to the capital. . . . Basic goods and foodstuffs, such as milk, oil, flour, sugar, butter, toilet paper, and the like were hard to find. Overall the paro [strike] had a devastating effect on the economy and on daily life." According to Oppenheim, the "paro forced many Chileans to choose sides. . . . The growing economic crisis was a major factor in turning people away from the UP [Allende's political party.]"

Unrest grew across the nation as inflation increased to more than 500 percent annually and food shortages multiplied. A strike erupted in the copper mines, which dragged on for weeks. Another strike broke out among bus drivers in Santiago.

Meanwhile, the Chilean military had begun to lose faith in the government. Many of Allende's supporters had been talking about disbanding the armed forces and substituting them with militia groups who were committed to the government's policies. In June, one military regiment led by Colonel Roberto Souper blockaded the presidential palace, called La Moneda. The coup attempt, however, was put down by military leaders who supported the government.

In July 1973, one of Allende's aides, naval Commander Arturo Araya, was assassinated. By this time the military had

In September 1973, the Chilean army, led by General Augusto Pinochet, over-threw Salvadore Allende as president, in what is now referred to as the Coup d'état of 1973. During the coup, Chilean jets bombed Allende's Moneda Palace where the president was found dead. In the photograph above, soldiers and firefighters carry the body of former president Salvador Allende out of the burned palace.

decided to act. Its leaders decided to force the defense minis-ter, General Carlos Prats, who was also head of the army, to resign. Prats believed that the Chilean military had a respon-sibility to support the elected government of Chile.

THE OVERTHROW OF ALLENDE

Michelle Bachelet's father, who by this time had become an air force general, agreed with Prats. Allende had asked General

"HISTORY IS OURS, AND THE PEOPLE OF THE WORLD WILL DETERMINE IT."

—Salvador Allende

Bachelet to lead the Chilean Food Distribution Office. This government agency was in charge of getting essential food to the Chilean people during strikes and shortages. Other military leaders, however, had decided that the time had come to take action against the government. The military had the support of the two major opposition groups, the National Party and the Christian Democrats. By August, these parties in the Chilean Congress passed a measure stating that Allende's programs were unconstitutional and calling on the military to take action. As Oppenheim wrote in *Politics in Chile,* "the two major parties of the opposition eventually came to the same basic conclusion: A military coup was necessary to resolve the political stalemate."

By September 1973, the Chilean military was prepared to strike. Early on the morning of September 11, Allende was told that military units had been called out of their barracks. Soon radio stations had fallen under control of army units. Allende had just time enough to issue a statement over the radio from Moneda palace. He knew the end was near. "Surely this will be my last opportunity to address you," Oppenheim's *Politics in Chile* reports that he told the Chilean people. "My words are not spoken in bitterness. I shall pay with my life for the loyalty of the people. . . . They [the military] have the might and they can enslave us, but they cannot halt the world's social progresses, not with crimes, nor with guns. History is ours, and the people of the world will determine it."

Allende remained at Moneda palace, which was bombed by three Chilean jets at about 11 a.m. Soldiers forced their way into the palace, which had been set afire by the bombing raid. Soon afterward, the body of Salvador Allende was brought out.

5

Chile's Military Government

DURING MOST OF ITS HISTORY, CHILE WAS UNDER MILITARY RULE FOR ONLY A short period. The new military government that took power in 1973, however, would remain in office for more than 15 years.

DEALING WITH TORTURE

The government was headed by the leaders of the Chilean army, the air force, the navy, and the national police. Michelle Bachelet had watched from the University of Santiago as the armed forces bombed the presidential palace and took control of the national government. She and other students at the university probably saw their new leaders appear on Chilean television the next evening. "We had to cut the cancer of Marxism from Chile," announced General Gustavo Leigh Guzmán, head of the air force. "Congress is closed until further notice. Political parties are in recess until further notice," added General Augusto Pinochet, head of the army and later president of Chile.

Augusto Pinochet is photographed days after he seized power from Salvadore Allende in 1973. Pinochet ruled as a military dictator of Chile from 1973 until 1990. When Patricio Aylwin was democratically elected president in 1990, a commission claimed that more than 2,200 people died during Pinochet's deadly regime.

For the military leaders, the first issue was eliminating all opposition to their new regime. Soldiers began rounding up politicians, union heads, and other Chilean citizens who had supported the Allende government. Many of them were immediately shot, while others were carried off to prison, where they were tortured.

Among those imprisoned was General Bachelet, Michelle's father. Although he had simply carried out his duties to the elected government of Chile, the leaders of the new military junta regarded him as a traitor. "His bank accounts were blocked, and they didn't let us take out money," Michelle

"THEY PUT FOUR OF US INSIDE A
CONTAINER NO BIGGER THAN A TABLE.
IN THE DARK, WE COULD HEAR
SCREAMS ALL DAY AND SOBBING ALL
NIGHT. IT WAS HOW I IMAGINED
HELL WOULD BE."

—Humberto Vergara

Bachelet was quoted as saying in a January 4, 2003, article in *The New York Times*, "When I walked down the street, people who had been very close to us crossed to the other side so as not to have to see us." General Bachelet was detained in the Santiago public prison, where he was repeatedly tortured. In March 1974, he suffered a severe heart attack brought on by the torture and died.

MICHELLE BACHELET IN PRISON

Early the following year, Michelle and her mother were taken to Villa Grimaldi—another prison in Santiago. This had been a luxurious estate before the military takeover. In *Torture and the Eucharist* by William T. Cavanaugh, former detainee Humberto Vergara, a peasant union official, said, "It was like a palace, with marble stairways and an indoor swimming pool. They put four of us inside a container no bigger than a table. In the dark, we could hear screams all day and sobbing all night. It was how I imagined hell would be. . . . The guards would splash in the pool and pass by the cells, saying they were going to kill this one or . . . that one."

The torture was carried out by the Directorate for National Intelligence (DINA), the new Chilean secret police. According to *Torture and the Eucharist*, "Disappearance and torture were important facets of the Pinochet regime's overall strategy, which aimed at dissolving all opposition social groups, such as [political] parties, church groups, unions, and community

"THEY KEPT TELLING HER THAT IF
SHE DIDN'T COLLABORATE [AND TELL
THEM ABOUT HER POLITICAL ACTIVI-
TIES BEFORE THE COUP] THEY WOULD
KILL HER MOTHER, BUT SHE
NEVER BROKE DOWN."

—Bachelet's cell mate

organizations." People lived in constant fear that they would be turned in by others in the community. The torture itself was designed to separate individuals from the rest of society and "reduce the prisoner to a condition of powerlessness. . . . Torture is intended to alter a person's identity, degrade him and strip him of human attributes but in most cases not to kill him." Instead the tortured victim was supposed to feel completely dependent on the state. The torture demonstrated the power of the new military government. When the torture finally stopped, it was designed to show that only the state had the ability to end the pain that a victim suffered.

As one victim recalled in *Torture and the Eucharist*, "I was arrested at about midnight on the 26th of December, 1975. Around 8 civilians arrived at my house, all armed with machine guns and small arms; after searching the house . . . they hand-cuffed me together with my wife, put tape over our eyes and dark glasses over that. . . . We were put into a private car . . . and taken to the Villa Grimaldi. They took us out of the car and immediately I was taken to the torture chamber. There they made me undress and with my hands and feet tied to the metal frame of the lower part of a bunk bed they began to apply electric current to me. This is the 'grill.' During the rest of the night they had me, applying electricity over my whole body, accompanied with sticks, because of which I came out with several fractured ribs. While they applied electricity they threw water on my whole body."

Michelle Bachelet *(center)* and her family observe a moment of silence at the grave of her father, General Alberto Bachelet in March 2006. When Augusto Pinochet seized power in 1973, military leaders who had supported the Allende government, such as Alberto Bachelet, were put in prison and tortured. In March 1974, Michelle Bachelet's father died of a heart attack after being severely tortured in prison.

Michelle Bachelet and her mother were subjected to torture as well. "They put tape and dark glasses over our eyes. We couldn't see," she recalled in a February 10, 2006, report by *Current Events*. Michelle was taken to Villa Grimaldi, while her mother was driven to another prison. In the March 2006 article "From Torture Victim to President" in *Progressive*, one of the women in the cell with Michelle said, "We could hear the screams from the torture chamber opposite our cell. She remained calm and tried to help us with her medical skills, singing with us in the afternoons, even though it annoyed the guards. They kept telling her that if she didn't collaborate [and tell them about her political activities before the coup] they would kill her mother, but she never broke down."

She remained in Villa Grimaldi for a month. "You can't just say that she was held for 30 days," Chilean professor Elizabeth Lira, an expert on the military regime, said in a *Women's eNews* report on November 20, 2005. "It was 30 days of total fear. Rape was frequent. Plus the punches, sexual abuse, denigration. They had very long interrogations and the use of electric current was common. You had to listen to others being tortured."

BACHELET LEAVES CHILE

Eventually Michelle and her mother were released, possibly because they still had friends in the military. They were forced into exile, like hundreds of others whom General Pinochet believed were a threat to the new regime. At first they went to Australia, where Michelle's brother, Alberto, had been living since the late 1960s. Eventually they left Australia and went to Communist East Germany.

East Germany had become a center for Chilean Socialists who were trying to begin an opposition movement against the military regime. Carlos Altamirano, the secretary-general of the Socialists, had escaped to East Germany soon after the military took power. According to reporter Jonathan Franklin in the November 2005 *Women's eNews* report, "Bachelet and her mother organized protests against the military junta that drew media attention and put pressure on the regime." Michelle's mother added, "We were more dangerous outside than inside Chile."

Meanwhile, Michelle continued her medical studies in East Germany, while working at a neighborhood health clinic.

Among the Chileans exiled to East Germany was an architect named Jorge Dávalos. Michelle and Dávalos were married in 1977 and had their first child, a boy named Sebastián, a year later.

THE MILITARY AND THE ECONOMY

Not only did the Pinochet government change the political situation in Chile, it also introduced new economic policies. Pinochet's primary goal was reducing inflation. He enlisted the support of a group of Chilean economists known as the Chicago Boys. These young men had attended Catholic University in Chile during the 1950s and 1960s. At that time, Catholic University had an exchange program with the University of Chicago in the United States. The young college students developed their economic principles at the University of Chicago under the direction of American economist Milton Friedman, who was a strong believer in the so-called "free market" economy. After their training in the United States, the Chilean economists returned home, where they taught free-market economics in Chile. Briefly stated, this approach urged the government to return all the state-owned businesses to private industry.

As the military regime took power in 1973, the Chicago Boys issued a plan called "the brick." This plan outlined their approach to taming inflation and fixing the Chilean economy. General Pinochet and his associates called in the Chicago Boys and decided to follow their approach to improve the Chilean economy. As a first step, Pinochet drastically reduced spending on government programs and stopped printing large amounts of money—two measures that began to reduce inflation. This "shock treatment," as it was called, threw thousands of Chileans out of work. Unemployment reached 20 percent by the end of 1975.

Meanwhile, the government began to sell the industries and banks that had been taken over by the Frei and Allende governments. These were bought up by groups of well-to-do Chileans who received easy credit from the banks, which they had also purchased. At the same time, the government lowered tariffs on imports and increased the value of the Chilean currency, the peso. As a result, foreign-made goods began flooding into Chile. Many Chileans borrowed money to buy expensive cars and other luxury items. In the countryside, the Pinochet government also made substantial changes. Land that had been redistributed to the poor was sold off to foreign agricultural companies that invested in the farms and developed a thriving fruit export business. Peasants, who had briefly owned their own land or worked for the government, went to work for the foreign companies.

According to free-market theories, if Chilean businesses were forced to compete with foreign products, they would become stronger. With tariffs reduced, however, many local companies went bankrupt. This only increased unemployment among middle-class people in Chilean society. For several years, bankrupt businesses and Chilean citizens continued to borrow, keeping the economy going. In 1981, however, the world economy fell into the grip of a recession—an economic downturn. Suddenly credit dried up, and the Chilean economy fell into a tailspin. Bankruptcies increased rapidly, and unemployment rose across the country.

POLITICS IN CHILE

Before the economic slowdown of the early 1980s, the Pinochet regime was unstoppable. Political opposition to the government was weak, and Pinochet had even decided to allow some exiles to return to Chile. Among them was Michelle Bachelet, her husband, her son, and her mother, who returned in 1979. As Michelle quickly saw, her country was controlled by a brutal dictatorship with no room for any Socialists like her. In 1980, Pinochet proposed a new constitution. Under the constitution, he would remain head of the

In 2006, Michelle Bachelet and Santiago's Mayor, Victor Barueto observe a memorial at Villa Grimaldi, a torture center used on political prisoners during Augusto Pinochet's dictatorship. Bachelet was imprisoned and tortured at Villa Grimaldi for 30 days in 1975.

government until a vote in 1989. Then Chileans would be asked to elect him to another eight years as president. Chile would run without a legislature until 1990, and no political parties were allowed to operate in the country. In addition, very little freedom of speech would be permitted.

After the new constitution was unveiled, Pinochet called for a yes-or-no vote, known as a *plebiscite*. He permitted a discussion of the constitution for 30 days before the vote. Although political parties had been banned, many people

As the rich became even richer, the poor fell further down the economic ladder.

spoke out against the new constitution. Among them was former President Eduardo Frei. The plebiscite was held in September 1980, and according to the results announced by the junta, two-thirds of the Chileans who voted had approved the constitution. Serious doubt, however, was cast on the accuracy of the results. As Lois Hecht Oppenheim wrote in *Politics in Chile*, "A state of exception, which prohibited public gatherings without official approval, was in effect for the entire country. Political parties did not legally exist, and the opposition camp had virtually no access to the mass media, particularly television. Finally, . . . those people designated to oversee the voting process and count the ballots at local precincts were Pinochet loyalists."

Although Pinochet seemed to be unbeatable, conditions began to change with the economic slowdown of the 1980s. In the years after the plebiscite, protests began to break out criticizing the military regime. Many of these protests were organized in barrios by community activists.

Under the economic programs of the Pinochet regime, poverty doubled. According to *Chile's Free-Market Miracle: A Second Look* by Joseph Collins and John Lear, as the rich became even richer, the poor fell further down the economic ladder. Even those who could find jobs were poorly paid and forced to work long hours. Real wages fell by over 40 percent during the 1980s, as noted in *Democracy and Poverty in Chile* by James Petras and Fernando Ignacio Leiva. According to one study, less than 50 percent of Chileans could afford to buy enough food to eat, *Chile's Free Market Miracle: A Second Look* reported. Therefore, many people needed help. Local self-help groups organized soup kitchens, where the poor could be fed. They also helped set up small businesses that made handicrafts and other products. Women in poor neighborhoods, or shantytowns, also played key roles in helping others. "The shantytown woman," according to *Democracy and Poverty in Chile*, "was the key actor in residential and local areas, acting as a central provider of social services, visiting the municipality in search of assistance, [and] caring for children."

Some of the activists operated under the sponsorship of the Catholic Church in Chile. Since most Chileans were Catholics, the Pinochet government hesitated to attack the Catholic Church. Catholic priests hid opponents of the military regime and spoke out against the junta. Labor unions also played a key role in the protest movement. Although they had few members and were officially outlawed, unions managed to remain in existence.

BACHELET'S ACTIVITIES UNDER THE DICTATORSHIP

Michelle Bachelet became involved with the protest movement, working behind the scenes against the Pinochet government. Meanwhile, she had finished her medical degree, concentrating in public health and pediatrics—medicine for children. In the days before the dictatorship, Chile had one of the most far-reaching health care programs in the world. Sixty-five percent of Chileans received free health care by the 1950s, according to *Chile's Free-Market Miracle: A Second Look*. This program had been expanded under the Frei and Allende governments. But the military regime drastically cut expenditures for public health. Many doctors who had supported Allende were put into prison or exiled. Chileans were encouraged to join privately run health maintenance organizations (HMOs). Many of the well-to-do could afford to join the HMOs and pay substantial fees for medical care, but the poor were left to receive treatment from an overworked and underfinanced public health system.

In addition to working in public health, Bachelet was also employed by an organization called Protection of Children Injured by States of Emergency Foundation (PIDEE), helping young people whose parents had been tortured, imprisoned, or killed during the military dictatorship. By 1984, she had given birth to a second child, Francisca. Shortly afterward, however, Michelle and her husband were separated. During the mid-1980s, she began a brief relationship with a member of a radical armed group dedicated to the overthrow of Pinochet. In 1986, this group made an unsuccessful attempt to assassinate him.

General Pinochet dealt with the growing unrest in Chile with a heavy hand. He turned out the army to put down the protests. The government realized, however, that it also had to take other steps to improve the economy. During the mid-1980s, the government stepped in and took over banks to save them from closing. Financial aid was also given to many businesses. Tariffs were raised to protect merchants, and the value of the peso was increased to reduce imports. The government also received financial help from international financial institutions like the World Bank and the International Monetary Fund. As a result, the economy slowly began to improve.

END OF THE CHILEAN DICTATORSHIP

Opposition to the government did not disappear, but continued to grow. General Pinochet planned a plebiscite for 1988, in which he expected to win a huge victory and continue as president for another eight years. Opposition groups, however, worked together to form an organization called Concertación por el No—Group for the No Vote. With only a short campaigning period, the Concertación had to work hard to defeat General Pinochet. But there was plenty of support for change among Chileans who had grown tired of an autocratic regime and a lagging economy.

Opposition supporters celebrate the defeat of General Augusto Pinochet in the 1988 election. Due to the formation of a coalition of opposition groups, nearly 55 percent of the electorate voted against the continuation of Pinochet's regime as dictator. Pinochet had no other choice than to step down as dictator, with Chile officially returning to a democractic state.

On October 5, 1988, Chileans went to the polls. In a stunning upset, Concertación received 55 percent of the vote to 44 percent for General Pinochet. Although the government was reluctant to admit the loss, Pinochet had no choice unless he wanted to risk civil war in Chile. He planned to step down as head of the government.

As a result of Pinochet's defeat, a campaign began to elect a new president of Chile in 1989. The Concertación became known as the *Concertación de Partidos por la Democracia*

(Coalition of Parties for Democracy). It included the Christian Democratic Party, the Socialists, and the Social Democratic Radical Party. Patricio Aylwin, who had been a leader of the Christian Democratic Party, was nominated to run for president. In addition, the Concertación nominated candidates to run for the Chilean Congress. Another candidate was Hernán Büchi. A former finance minister in the Pinochet government, he was supported by conservatives. The third candidate was a millionaire businessman, Francisco Javier Errázuriz. The election, held on December 14, 1989, gave the victory to Aylwin, who received 55 percent of the vote. Concertación candidates also took a majority of seats in the Chamber of Deputies and the Senate.

The victory of the Concertación not only changed Chile, but also the political future of Michelle Bachelet.

6

Bachelet and the Democratic Government

CHILE RETURNED TO DEMOCRATIC GOVERNMENT IN 1989. PRESIDENT Aylwin took the oath of office as president at the National Congress, a building recently completed in Valparaíso. But the Pinochet years were not immediately forgotten.

THE AYLWIN ADMINISTRATION

A presidential commission appointed by President Aylwin, called the Commission of Truth and Reconciliation, reported that more than 2200 Chileans had been executed by Pinochet's regime. Mass graves had been discovered containing the bodies of some of those victims killed by the military and the national police during Pinochet's rule. As a result, many Chileans wanted the military leaders brought to trial for the killings they had ordered.

In 1978, however, the government had established an Amnesty Law prohibiting anyone from being tried who had committed a human rights violation between 1973 and 1978. President Aylwin decided to ignore the Amnesty Law. Instead, he proclaimed the Aylwin Doctrine, calling for those who had violated human rights to be brought to trial. Trials of former Pinochet government officials began during the 1990s. In 1993, for example, General Manuel Contreras, former head of DINA, was convicted of human rights abuses and sentenced to prison.

Meanwhile, President Aylwin had to struggle to run a government that was not entirely under his control. During his years in office, General Pinochet had filled the bureaucracy with his appointees. In addition, judges in the Chilean courts had been appointed by Pinochet. Pinochet had also banned any municipal elections, appointing all the city mayors himself. All of these bureaucrats and politicians still remained in office.

In addition, General Pinochet remained head of the Chilean army. The army was independent from the elected president. President Aylwin, along with many Chileans, wanted Pinochet to resign his position, but he refused to leave. The constitution of 1980 permitted him to remain in charge of the army until 1997. In addition, the constitution allowed Pinochet to hold significant political power within the Chilean Congress. He was given the right to appoint nine senators. These men helped give the Conservatives a majority of votes in the Chilean Senate. As a result, they could block legislation proposed by the Liberal Aylwin government. Aylwin, however, did succeed in democratizing local elections. While Conservatives who controlled the Senate refused to permit mayors to be elected, they did agree that town councils, who were elected by the voters, should choose the mayors.

THE ECONOMY

The economic recovery—which had begun under Pinochet—continued during the 1990s. The prosperous economy grew at

7 percent to 10 percent per year. This was much higher than other Latin American economies, and Chile became known as the "jaguar of South America." Tariffs were reduced from 15 percent under the Pinochet regime to 8 percent. This encouraged foreign investment, especially from the United States, and Chilean exports increased. While copper still made up 40 percent of these exports, they also included fruit, lumber, wine, and fish. For example, according to Lois Hecht Oppenheim's *Politics in Chile*, Chile has become the second largest producer of salmon in the world.

Most of the economic growth, however, did not help the Chilean poor, who still made up about 25 percent of the population. Nevertheless, the government succeeded in raising wages among workers. In addition, Aylwin passed new taxes that were aimed at paying for increased social services to the poor. These included greater expenditures on the public health programs.

During the 1990s, Michelle Bachelet was working for the Ministry of Health in Santiago. Her patients were among the poor Chileans who could not afford the private HMOs. Chile had also been struck by an outbreak of acquired immune deficiency syndrome (AIDS). This disease attacks an individual's immune system, breaking down the body's defenses and causing death. In addition to her service in public health, Bachelet worked for the Chilean National AIDS Commission. There she began a relationship with Dr. Aníbal Henríquez, and in 1992 gave birth to her third child, a daughter named Sofía. Meanwhile, Bachelet's work in public health led to an appointment as senior assistant to the deputy health minister in 1994.

THE FREI GOVERNMENT

That same year, Eduardo Frei Ruiz-Tagle was sworn in as president of Chile. A leader of Concertación, Frei was the son of Eduardo Frei, the Christian Democrat who had been elected president in the 1960s. In the 1993 presidential election, he easily defeated the candidate of the Conservative parties, Arturo Alessandri, as well as several other opponents. Under Frei's government, the Chilean economy continued to grow. "The combination of stable civilian government and free-market economics made Chile a favorite target of foreign investors," author Robert Buckman wrote in *Latin America.*

Nevertheless, the Pinochet issue did not disappear. Although General Pinochet resigned as head of the army in 1998, he did not leave politics. The constitution of 1980 had given him a lifetime seat as one of the appointed senators in the Chilean Senate. Pinochet took up this position soon after leaving the army.

THE PINOCHET CASE

In 1998, Pinochet traveled to Great Britain to have a delicate operation performed on his back. While in London, a judge in Spain issued a warrant for Pinochet's arrest. The charge was the torture and murder of Spanish citizens living in Chile during the Pinochet regime. Judge Baltasar Garzón of Spain ruled that these were crimes against humanity. Although Pinochet had not been arrested by the Chilean government, it made no difference. Judge Garzón said that because of Pinochet's crimes, he could stand trial anywhere in the world.

Pinochet was forced to remain in Great Britain under house arrest—that is, he had to stay confined inside a house in London, the English capital. Meanwhile, the English courts tried to determine whether Pinochet should be sent to Spain to stand trial. Although many Chileans did not like Pinochet, they were opposed to another country telling Chile how to handle crimes that had been committed inside its borders.

Finally, the British government decided that Pinochet was not mentally stable enough to stand trial. Instead he was sent back to Chile early in 2000. Home in Chile, Pinochet's problems did not end. As a senator for life, he could not be forced to stand trial under Chilean law. Nevertheless, the Supreme

Chilean students hold a mock "Diploma of Terror" accusing former General Augusto Pinochet of human rights violations during his regime as dictator. When Chile returned to democratic rule under President Patricio Aylwin in 1990, the Commission of Truth and Reconciliation reported that more than 2,200 Chileans had been murdered under Pinochet's dictatorship.

Court of Chile decided that there were exceptions to the law. Although the law covered certain crimes, kidnapping was not among them. The court ruled that Pinochet had ordered the kidnapping of Chilean citizens after the coup. These innocent Chileans were arrested by army soldiers and never seen again. Pinochet's lawyers tried to prove that the former general was not mentally capable of standing trial in Chile. Meanwhile, he had resigned from the Senate in 2002.

The legal issues involving Pinochet continued. In 2003, Pinochet was interviewed on a television program and did not appear to be incompetent. The following year, the Chilean

> ## "IN A CERTAIN WAY
> ## I WAS RE-ENCOUNTERING PART
> ## OF MY ROOTS, WHICH HAD BEEN
> ## SEVERED DURING THAT PART OF OUR
> ## HISTORY IN WHICH OUR SOCIETY
> ## WAS SO POLARIZED."
>
> —Michelle Bachelet

Supreme Court once again voted that he was competent to stand trial. In the meantime, Pinochet was also being investigated for fraud, bribery, and tax evasion. These charges involved approximately $27 million that he was accused of depositing in secret bank accounts. Early in 2006, charges were also brought against Pinochet's wife and children for being involved in the same alleged scheme. Later that year, the Chilean Supreme Court ordered that Pinochet should stand trial for murders he was accused of ordering while president. Late in 2006, the former dictator suffered a severe heart attack and died.

BACHELET AND A NEW PRESIDENT

While the controversy over General Pinochet was still raging in Chile, Michelle Bachelet had taken a new direction in her career—one that brought her into military affairs. In 1996, she enrolled in the National Academy for Strategic Policy Studies. There she studied relationships between the military and the elected politicians in Chile. In part she was following in her father's footsteps. "In a certain way I was re-encountering part of my roots, which had been severed during that part of our history [Pinochet's regime] in which our society was so polarized," she said in a *New York Times* article by Larry Rohter. "Most people with my background feel a profound rejection towards anything that has to do with the military, but I felt like I was recovering part of my being." Bachelet also

Ricardo Lagos *(above)* waves to supporters during the 1999 presidential election. After serving as minister of education during Patricio Aylwin's presidency and then as minister of public works during Eduardo Frei Ruiz-Tagle's presidency, Lagos narrowly won the presidential election in 1999. When he assumed his role as president, Lagos appointed Michelle Bachelet as his minister of health.

wanted to understand how to prevent a military overthrow from happening again. Graduating at the top of her class, she went to the United States on a scholarship to study at the

Inter-American Defense College. After returning to Chile, she became an aide to the Chilean defense minister in 1998. Soon afterward, she attended the Chilean War Academy, the same place where Pinochet had taught earlier during his military career.

In 1999, Chileans went to the polls to elect a new president. The candidate of the Concertación was Ricardo Lagos, while the Conservative parties nominated Joaquín Lavín. In 1996, Lavín had been elected mayor of a suburb of Santiago. One of the candidates who ran against him was Michelle Bachelet, although she received only a small number of votes. A recent downturn in the economy had turned some voters against Concertación. The presidential election was very tight, with neither Lavín nor Lagos receiving a majority of votes. Several other candidates had participated in the election, denying either Lavín or Lagos a majority. In a runoff election in January 2000, Lagos was elected. Bachelet worked in the Lagos campaign, helping him to achieve victory. Soon after he became president, Lagos appointed Bachelet minister of health. The major focus of her work was improving Chile's public health system.

BACHELET AND THE LAGOS GOVERNMENT

Under the Lagos administration, the economy began to improve. Indeed by 2005, it was growing at a rate of more than 6 percent a year. This was due to high demand for copper, especially in China, which was rapidly expanding its economy. As a result of higher demand, copper prices rose rapidly, increasing revenues to the government. In addition, exports of other products, such as wine, increased.

While the economy was growing, however, President Lagos was forced to confront problems in other areas. Among them was the ongoing issue of how to deal with General Pinochet. In addition, a scandal broke out as newspapers began to

In the photograph above, President Ricardo Lagos shakes hands with former minister of health, Michelle Bachelet, after she is sworn in as the new minister of defense in 2002. When Michelle Bachelet was appointed to her new position, she became the first woman in Latin America to become minister of defense.

report in 2002 that air force officers were trying to prevent investigations into abuses during the Pinochet regime. These investigations had continued for the decade and a half since Pinochet had left power.

"I STUDIED MEDICINE BECAUSE I
WANTED TO SERVE AND HELP OTHERS.
I AM CONVINCED THAT THE DUTY
OF DEFENSE IS TO MAINTAIN PEACE
AND AVOID WAR."

—Michelle Bachelet

By this time, President Lagos had appointed Michelle Bachelet to a new position—defense minister. She was the first woman in Latin America to hold such a post. "I studied medicine because I wanted to serve and help others," she was quoted as saying a January 4, 2003, *New York Times* article. "I am convinced that the duty of defense is to maintain peace and avoid war."

As defense minister, Bachelet said in a January 25, 2006, interview on PBS's *Online NewsHour* that she had begun "to build bases in our society where tolerance, understanding of diversity, integration and not discrimination will be the main policies." This involved "reconciliation between people who were victims and their families and people who were responsible for that." She added that, because she had suffered under the Pinochet military regime, "I felt I could serve as a bridge between the military and civil society." She said she also realized, however, that "I have to do my best to create . . . conditions in our country in order that we will be able to guarantee to further generations that they will never have to live what we had to live."

In order to accomplish this goal, Bachelet worked with the commander-in-chief of the Chilean army, General Juan Emilio Cheyre. General Cheyre issued a declaration in 2003 promising that "never again" would the military undermine the elected government of Chile. Bachelet also recognized that reconciliation would take work, and the trials of Pinochet's former henchmen had to continue. "I'm a doctor," she was quoted as

I HAVE TO DO MY BEST TO CREATE ... CONDITIONS IN OUR COUNTRY IN ORDER THAT WE WILL BE ABLE TO GUARANTEE TO FURTHER GENERATIONS THAT THEY WILL NEVER HAVE TO LIVE WHAT WE HAD TO LIVE.

—Michelle Bachelet

saying in a March 9, 2006, article in *Spiegel,* "so allow me to use a medical analogy to explain the problem: Only cleaned wounds can heal, otherwise they'll keep opening up again, and will likely become infected and begin to fester. It's clear to me that the truth must be brought to light."

The trials continued under President Lagos. As Bachelet was quoted as saying in *Progressive* in March 2006, some Chileans want to forget what happened, but she is not one of them. "I will never support any law that would pardon military personnel accused of committing human rights abuses during the dictatorship. . . . Chile is now on the right path, but much more needs to be done."

7

President of Chile

IN 2005, MICHELLE BACHELET TOOK THE NEXT STEP IN HER POLITICAL career and ran for the office of president of Chile. In an interview published March 9, 2006, by *Spiegel* after her election, she said, "What's most important to me is to be able to fulfill the hopes of as many citizens as possible." She added: "Chileans expect me to pay more attention to social justice and bring more democracy to the country."

PROTESTS OVER EDUCATION

After her election, early in 2006, she began to focus on some of the issues that she had discussed during the campaign. One of these issues was education for the poor. As a candidate, Bachelet had promised to improve the lot of Chile's poor, who still compose a large part of the population. Impatient with the pace at which the government was

Bachelet's supporters rally to celebrate the victory of the first female to ever win the presidency in Chile. As a divorced, single mother who has openly talked about being an agnostic, Michelle Bachelet was unlike any former presidential candidate. But, in 2006 Bachelet changed the face of Chilean politics when she won the majority of the vote.

**APPROXIMATELY 700,000 HIGH
SCHOOL STUDENTS LEFT CLASSES
TO DEMAND THAT THE BACHELET
ADMINISTRATION SPEND MORE
MONEY ON PUBLIC EDUCATION.**

moving, however, students went on strike on May 30, 2006. Approximately 700,000 high school students left classes to demand that the Bachelet administration spend more money on public education. The government ordered the police to step in and break up the demonstrations. Many of the protesters were arrested, although police resorted to beatings to stop some rock-throwing demonstrators. After talks with the government broke down, the student strike continued. With worldwide prices for copper soaring, the strikers demanded that President Bachelet spend some of the government's large copper revenues on education. They wanted more teachers, new school buildings, and free bus rides to school.

President Bachelet responded by promising a $135 million new program to improve public schools. This included school construction as well as free lunches for students who cannot afford them. "The state will be the guarantor of a quality education for all Chileans to be able to study in dignified conditions," she was quoted as saying in a June 4, 2006, *New York Times* article. When the strikers received her offer, however, they rejected it and continued to strike. "In a democracy, everyone has the right to mobilize," President Bachelet said. "But the truth is that this is the maximum the government can offer. The reforms will go ahead with or without a strike."

Bachelet, however, did decide to go a step further. In addition to a new funding program, she organized a 60-person committee to evaluate public education. Among its members were high school and college students as well as teachers and experts in higher education. Striking students agreed to

During her presidential campaign, Michelle Bachelet had promised to improve Chile's public education system. In 2006, Chilean students, upset with the administration's lack of educational reform, participated in a national strike. In this 2006 photograph, students carry their chairs and desks during protests in Santiago, Chile. Michelle Bachelet responded to the massive outcry by promising $135 million to improve public schools.

consider the proposal. "The president's panel doesn't exactly fulfill all our expectations, but it is a reasonable advance," one of the students leading the strikes was quoted as saying by The Associated Press on June 7, 2006. "The number of spots given the high school students is too few. But perhaps things can be worked out. Personally for me this is progress."

> **"BEING A WOMAN WAS AN ADVANTAGE WHILE MS. BACHELET WAS A CANDIDATE.... NOW ALL THE GOVERNMENT'S PROBLEMS ARE BEING ATTRIBUTED TO THE FACT THAT SHE'S A WOMAN."**
> —Marcela Rios

Some critics believed that Bachelet was too weak in dealing with the student protesters. "The government should put its trousers on," some have said—criticizing Bachelet's programs because she is a woman. As one observer, Marcela Rios, was quoted as saying in an August 12, 2006, article in the *Economist*, "Being a woman was an advantage while Ms. Bachelet was a candidate. . . . Now all the government's problems are being attributed to the fact that she's a woman."

Following the strikes, President Bachelet left for the United States, where she met with President George W. Bush. Referring to her visit, Bachelet was quoted in a June 7, 2006, *New York Times* article as saying that Chile and the United States "share fundamental values and principles about democratic development with an open economy, and a respect for human rights." After returning to Chile, President Bachelet continued with other programs that she had discussed during the election. These included the construction of day care centers that would help working mothers care for their children.

WOMEN IN CHILE

Many women have hoped that Bachelet's election might improve the status of females in Chile. Women in Chile lag behind those in other Latin American nations. For example, only 15 percent of the elected representatives in Chile's Congress are women, compared to more than 30 percent in Costa Rica and Argentina. Chilean women also earn less than men for comparable jobs. Their paychecks are about 19 percent smaller. With its heavy

In 2006, miners who worked for government-owned copper company, Codelco, went on a 25-day strike for higher wages. With Chile producing a large percentage of the world's copper supply, the miners demanded better treatment and increased pay. In the photograph above, more than 1,000 miners march in 2006.

reliance on mining, Chile has not made a major effort to promote the growth of other economic areas. As one American banker, Kathleen Barclay, was quoted as saying in *Economist* on August 12, 2006, "Chile is throwing talent out the window at a rate that is exponentially damaging to the economy." Before she was even a candidate for president, Bachelet noted her aims in this area, telling *The New York Times* for a January 4, 2003, article: "Chilean women have the capacity to do anything, and I believe that Chile is going to offer even more opportunities to its women. It would be a shame for the country to waste that ability in any field."

During her first year in office, President Bachelet appointed a cabinet that was 50 percent women—10 out of 20 cabinet ministers—a significant break from governments of the past. She has also considered introducing legislation requiring political parties to nominate more women to run in congressional elections. "We'd like it to be 50% but haven't decided yet," her minister for women's affairs, Laura Albornoz, was quoted as saying in the August 12, 2006, *Economist* article.

MINERS' STRIKE

In August 2006, however, Bachelet's focus shifted to a major crisis in Chile. With copper revenues so large, miners wondered about their piece of the pie. Miners at the copper company Escondida went on strike for higher wages. The strike at Escondida's biggest mine lasted 25 days when the government finally agreed to a 5 percent wage hike. In addition, the miners were given healthy bonuses as well as improved health benefits. This seemed to reflect President Bachelet's promise to improve the lives of Chile's working people. The agreement, however, brought concern from other mining companies in Chile that the government had given the miners too much. The agreement may affect other sectors of the economy, too. Government workers may demand higher wage increases to keep pace with the miners.

HEALTH ISSUES

In September 2006, President Bachelet faced a crisis in health care—an area that was especially important to her. Chilean Health Minister Dr. María Soledad Barría announced that teenage girls would be given access to contraception pills

As president, Michelle Bachelet has dealt with many challenges including natural disasters, health care crises, and student demonstrations. Although her position comes with great difficulty, Michelle Bachelete continues to serve as positive leader.

at health clinics. The so-called morning-after pill would become available to girls 14 and older. Contraception was expected to help reduce pregnancies among teenagers in Chile, who bear 15 percent of the nation's newborns. But this decision created a furor among Conservative politicians and leaders of the Catholic Church in Chile. In a September 16, 2006, article in the *Economist*, the Catholic Church said the plan "recalls the public policies of totalitarian regimes that wanted to impose regulation on people's intimate lives." As a result, a Chilean court stopped the policy from taking effect, at least temporarily.

Meanwhile, natural disasters struck Chile as floods and landslides gripped the south. The government was criticized for not responding adequately to these disasters and providing relief for Chileans caught up in them. As a result, President Bachelet was forced to make changes in her cabinet. The minister of the interior as well as other officials were replaced. Chilean presidents usually do not make cabinet changes so early in their administrations, but President Bachelet believed that she had no choice.

It was a difficult beginning for the first woman president of Chile. Indeed, by early 2007, a poll in Chile indicated that more than 60 percent of the population no longer had faith in President Bachelet's ability to lead the country. One reason was a declining economy, where growth fell to 4 percent from 5.7 percent a year earlier. Another reason was a new bus system in Santiago that did not have a sufficient number of buses and bus lanes. Bachelet apologized to the Chilean people. Then, to deal with this issue, she fired her minister of transportation and appointed a new one, Rene Cortazar. The president also made other changes in her cabinet.

Meanwhile, Bachelet opened 800 new child care centers and increased the number of people covered by the government's health care program. These measures fulfilled promises that she had made during her presidential campaign. Nevertheless, the early part of her administration received a mixed report card from most Chileans. They were looking for President Bachelet to do better and satisfy the hopes that many voters had placed in her when she was elected.

Chronology

1818	Chile becomes independent republic.
	Bernardo O'Higgins becomes head of government.
1830s	Chilean leaders write new constitution.
	Diego Portales governs Chile.
1884	War of the Pacific; Chile defeats Peru and Bolivia.
1891	Civil war in Chile.
1891–1925	Parliamentary republic in Chile.
1920	Arturo Alessandri elected president of Chile.
1925	Chilean leaders write a new constitution.
1927	Carlos Ibáñez imposes a military dictatorship.
1931	Ibáñez resigns during Great Depression.
1932	Alessandri returns as president.
1938	Pedro Cerda elected president.
1941–1952	Juan Ríos and Gabriel Videla serve as presidents of Chile.
1951	Michelle Bachelet born in Santiago, Chile.
1952	Ibáñez returns as president.
1958	Jorge Alessandri becomes president of Chile.
1962–63	Michelle Bachelet lives in United States.
1964	Eduardo Frei elected president.
1970	Michelle Bachelet enters University of Chile.
	Socialist Salvador Allende elected president of Chile.

1973	Allende overthrown by military; General Augusto Pinochet heads new government.
1975	Michelle Bachelet and mother imprisoned and tortured by new government; exiled from Chile; go to East Germany.
1977	Michelle Bachelet married in East Germany.
1978	Bachelet has first child.
1979	Bachelet and family return to Chile.
1984	Bachelet gives birth to second child; works in public health field; she and husband separate
1988	Pinochet defeated in plebiscite.
1989	Patricio Aylwin elected president.
1990s	Bachelet works for Ministry of Health.
1992	Eduardo Frei becomes president; Bachelet has third child.
1996	Bachelet enrolls at National Academy of Strategic Studies.
1998	Bachelet becomes aide to Chilean defense minister.
1999	Ricardo Lagos elected president.
2000	Bachelet becomes minister of health.
2002	Bachelet becomes defense minister.
2005	Bachelet runs for president of Chile.
2006	Michelle Bachelet elected president of Chile. Bachelet deals with strike among students. Bachelet settles miners' strike.

BIBLIOGRAPHY

BOOKS

Buckman, Robert. *Latin America.* Harpers Ferry, W.Va.: Stryker-Post Publications, 2005.

Castillo-Feliú, Guillermo I. *Culture and Customs of Chile.* Westport, CT: Greenwood Press, 2000.

Cavanaugh, William T. *Torture and the Eucharist.* Malden, MA: Blackwell Publishers, 1998.

Collier, Simon, and William Sater. *A History of Chile, 1808– 1994.* New York: Cambridge University Press, 1996.

Collins, Joseph, and John Lear. *Chile's Free-Market Miracle: A Second Look.* Oakland, Calif. The Institute for Food and Development, 1995.

Department of the Army. *Chile: A Country Study.* Washington, D.C., 1994.

Oppenheim, Lois Hecht. *Politics in Chile.* Boulder, Colo.: Westview Press, 1999.

Petras, James, and Fernando Leiva. *Democracy and Poverty in Chile: The Limits to Electoral Politics.* Boulder, Colo.: West- view Press, 1994.

MAGAZINE AND NEWSPAPER ARTICLES

"A Difficult Pill to Swallow." *The Economist,* September 16, 2006.

"Chile's Bachelet Moves to Defuse Protests." *Associated Press,* June 7, 2006.

Daniels, Alfonso. "From Torture Victim to President." *Progressive,* March 2006.

Franklin, Jonathan. "Chile's Michelle Bachelet Poised for Presidency." *Women's eNews,* November 20, 2005.

Gustavo Gonzalez. "Bachelet Makes History, Marks Cultural Shift." *Inter Press Service News Agency,* January 16, 2006.

"Interview with Michelle Bachelet: 'Only Cleaned Wounds Can Heal.'" *Spiegel,* March 9, 2006.

"La Presidenta Bachelet." *Current Events,* February 10, 2006.

"Left Behind." *The Economist,* August 12, 2006.

Moreno, Felipe. "Chile's Economy and the New President." *Contemporary Review,* March 2006.

Monte Reel. "Female, Agnostic and the Next Presidente?" *Washington Post Foreign Service,* December 10, 2005.

Larry Rohter. "Chilean Promised a New Deal; Now Striking Youth Demand It." *The New York Times,* June 4, 2006.

Rohter, Larry. "A Leader Making Peace with Chile's Past." *The New York Times,* January 16, 2006.

Rohter, Larry. "Jailed by Pinochet, She Now Runs the Military." *The New York Times,* January 4, 2003.

Rohter, Larry. "Visit to U.S. Not a First for Chile's First Female President." *The New York Times,* June 7, 2006.

"The Unexpected Travails of the Woman Who Would be President." *The Economist,* December 10, 2005.

Vincent, Isabel. "A Continental Shift to the Left." *Maclean's,* January 16, 2006.

"Will Michelle Bachelet Help Women or Hinder Them?" *The Economist,* August 12, 2006.

"Writing the Next Chapter in a Latin American Success Story." *The Economist,* April 2, 2005.

WEB SITES

BellaOnline: The Voice of Women. "Michelle Bachelet, President and Single Mom," Available online. http://www .bellaonline.com/articles/art17426.asp.

BBC News. "The Woman Taking Chile's Top Job," Available online. http://news.bbc.co.uk/1/hi/world/americas/ 4087510.stm.

Espíndola, Roberto. "Michelle Bachelet: Chile's Next President?" OpenDemocracy, Free Thinking for the World. Available online. http://www.opendemocracy.net/debates/ article.jsp?id=3&debateId=33&articleId=3097.

Malamud, Carlos. "Michelle Bachelet's Victory and the Political Future of Chile," NuevaMayoria.com. Available online. March 7, 2006.

Online NewsHour. "An Interview with Chile's New President-Elect," Available online. Available online. http://www.pbs .org/newshour/bb/latin_america/jan-june06/chile_ 1-25.html. January 25, 2006.

Richardson, Charlene. "Diego Portales: A Chilean Biography," Historical Text Archive. Available online. http://historicaltextarchive.com/sections.php?op= viewarticle&artid=425.

FURTHER READING

Brown, Jonathan C. *A Brief History of Argentina.* New York: Facts on File, 2002.

Crooker, Richard A. *Chile.* New York: Chelsea House, 2004.

Fearns, Les and Daisy. *Argentina.* New York: Facts on File, 2005.

Galvin, Irene. *Chile: Land of Poets and Patriots.* Minneapolis: Dillon Press, 1990.

McNair, Sylvia. *Chile.* New York: Children's Press, 2000.

Morrison, Marion. *Chile.* New York: Facts on File, 2006.

Winter, Jane Kohen. *Chile.* Tarrytown, N.Y.: Marshall Cavendish, 2002.

PHOTO CREDITS

INDEX

About the Authors

RICHARD WORTH is the author of more than 50 books, including the Chelsea House titles *Independence for Latino America* (Latino-American History), *Dalai Lama* (Spiritual Leaders and Thinkers), *Dolores Huerta* (The Great Hispanic Heritage) and *Gangs and Crime* (Crime, Justice, And Punishment), which was selected to the New York Public Library's Books for the Teen Age list in 2003.

ARTHUR M. SCHLESINGER, JR. is remembered as the leading American historian of our time. He won the Pulitzer Prize for his books *The Age of Jackson* (1945) and *A Thousand Days* (1965), which also won the National Book Award. Professor Schlesinger was the Albert Schweitzer Professor of the Humanities at the City University of New York and was involved in several other Chelsea House projects, including the series *Revolutionary War Leaders*, *Colonial Leaders*, and *Your Government.*

ML

6/09